ADHD Toolkit for Women

(2 Books in 1)

Workbook & Guide to Overcome ADHD Challenges
and Win at Life

Sarah Davis
&
Linda Hill

i

Table of Contents

Table of Contents

BOOK # 1

Women with ADHD

The Complete Guide to Stay Organized, Overcome
Distractions, and Improve Relationships.

Manage Your Emotions, Finances, and Succeed in Life

Introduction

"A woman is in full circle. Within her is the power to create, nurture and transform."
~ Diane Mariechild

As a woman, society expects a lot out of you. You expect a lot out of yourself. If you are a mother and a wife, you take care of yourself, but you also take care of the lives of your family. If you are single and career-oriented, you work hard and do your best to show how much an asset you are to your chosen company. If you are anything in between, you still provide a great amount to society, and it is rarely recognized.

This ideology of women can be enough to put enough pressure on anyone's shoulders, but sometimes you know when something isn't working right inside yourself. Still, you aren't sure what it is. That pressure can balloon into some major anxiety.

Seeking out the help of a professional can give your mind a little bit of ease, but what happens when your trusted professional says they believe you have ADHD?

Do you scoff, do you question, do you flat out deny that is what could be up with your brain? Do you think that if you were going to be diagnosed with Attention Deficit Hyperactivity Disorder, you would have to be a child?

Those reactions are common, and getting diagnosed as an adult is becoming a more natural phenomenon than you may realize.

However, an ADHD diagnosis may be a harder pill to swallow.

When you think of ADHD, your first inclination might be to think of adolescent boys who run all over the place and cannot seem to pay attention to anything.

That is the current stereotype, anyway.

ADHD can be diagnosed at any age in any gender. The most misdiagnosed of all people with ADHD are women and girls. ADHD affects roughly five percent of adults in the United States. Four out of every ten teachers have reported that ADHD symptoms are harder to recognize in girls. And now, by adulthood, because ADHD has gone untreated in women, most have one or more comorbidity disorders, which can add complications to ADHD. Comorbidity disorders are another issue that has co-mingled with one disorder already. Those with ADHD tend to have bipolar disorder, anxiety, or depression.

While women and girls are the most under-diagnosed with ADHD, women from age twenty-four to thirty-six are now the fastest-growing population diagnosed and treated for ADHD.

While you may be slightly familiar with ADHD, you may not care much about it until someone suggests that you could have it. If you are an adult, you may never have even thought that ADHD could be a possibility because you are not physically overactive, but maybe your brain is.

There are three main symptoms of Attention Deficit Hyperactivity Disorder (ADHD).

1. **Inattention** — Where you are unable to focus.

2. **Hyperactivity** — Where your mind or body produces excess thoughts or movement that happens at unsuitable times.

3. **Impulsivity** — When you act on a thought without assessing the consequences.

So, why are women harder to diagnose?

Women and girls with ADHD have symptoms that present a little differently than the more commonly known symptoms. Another reason is how women will compensate for the disorder without even realizing it.

Unfortunately, although ADHD has been reported for over 200 years, research hasn't done much about how gender and ADHD mix together. Instead, studies have focused on the symptoms that are easier to see.

Women tend to have internalized symptoms such as inattention, anxiety, and depression. The compensatory behaviors that women develop can even mask ADHD. Eventually, a woman who offsets her ADHD symptoms with other mechanisms can be called a perfectionist, which will help her cope with feeling inadequate. Still, this method can be maladaptive and heighten anxiety in the woman instead of providing her with healthy coping skills.

Although there are gaps in the ADHD knowledge between genders, a woman needs to know what ADHD looks like on her. It's also important for her family to understand what she is going through. Several factors can make life a bit harder, such as how the woman presents herself, how she copes, and constant misunderstandings that add extra challenges to an already stressful experience.

So, that is all the bad news.

The good news is that once you or your counselor suspects you have ADHD, you can begin to help yourself, even before your formal diagnosis.

This book has a plethora of information, knowledge, and data about ADHD, and it has been designed specifically just for you, a woman with ADHD. There are resources at the back of this book so you can check out other places to help yourself.

You are a smart, strong, and intelligent woman. Your ADHD is not who you are. It's just a part of you—and it is very manageable. I will help you lay down a foundation so that you can take on ADHD and guide yourself into a new way of living life. This way will include relationships (romantic and platonic), socialization, work, school, finances, health, and more. You can mold your routine into the life you want and start strong.

Just because you'll be working with your ADHD instead of against it doesn't mean you won't have some hard times. There will be days when you want to give up or when your anxiety becomes so much that you feel as though you're doing something wrong. I'm here to tell you now, and even then, you're not doing anything wrong. You're doing it all right.

If you jumped into a routine and didn't have a few bumps along the way, it isn't changing enough in your life. This book will teach you how to create a stable relationship with ADHD, help you admonish bad habits developed throughout the years, and show you how to accept all parts of yourself.

You don't have to do any of this alone. I am here to guide you through this process and look forward to walking with you on your journey with ADHD.

CHAPTER ONE

What Is ADHD?

"One of the most courageous things you can do is identify yourself, know who you are, what you believe in and where you want to go."
~ *Sheila Murray Bethel*

Introduction

Attention Deficit Hyperactivity Disorder or ADHD is a neurodevelopmental disorder. Neurodevelopment is how your brain develops neurological paths, which can influence how you function and perform. These functions can include attention, critical thinking, focusing, memory, reading abilities, etc. Each time you learn something, you create new pathways in your brain, improving your neurodevelopment.

As your neurodevelopment improves, your brain's structure will keep the information you've learned.

However, when you are diagnosed with ADHD, the neurodevelopment of your brain doesn't work the same way as those who don't have ADHD. Attention Deficit Hyperactivity Disorder is one of the most common disorders in the population.

Symptoms

Symptoms of ADHD include hyperactivity, impulsivity, and inattention.

ADHD is diagnosed by medical professionals such as a psychiatrist.

If you've experienced five or more of the following symptoms for longer than six months, it is a good idea to reach out to a therapist and tell them your concerns, so you're able to get tested.

Check off the following symptoms that seem like you:

Inattentiveness

- Can't pay attention to details and makes careless mistakes at your job.

- Have issues with focus, such as staying on task or finishing activities, especially during conversations, reading, and lectures.

- Have problems following through on duties for your job.

- Have been accused of not listening during conversations.

- Have issues organizing your day—cannot manage time well. You often miss deadlines or have been told your work is disorganized or messy.

- Dislike or avoid projects that may require continued mental effort, like completing forms and preparing reports.

- Often lose important items that you need daily. Items like cellphones, glasses, keys, wallets, etc.

- You become distracted easily.

- You forget about daily tasks like chores, errands, keeping appointments, paying bills, and returning phone calls.

Hyperactivity or Impulsiveness

- Have issues sitting still. Often jiggles feet or hands, shifts in your seat, or fidgets.

- Have an inability to stay seated at work.

- Need to be "on the go" constantly.

- Talk too much.

- Are unable to do quiet activities.

- You cannot seem to wait for someone to finish asking a question before you are finishing their sentences or answering. You cannot wait to speak.

- Interrupts other conversations, games, activities, etc., without being asked to join. Or, you may take over an activity completely to avoid having to give instructions or explain yourself.

If you have five or more checkmarks above, you can take the list and show it to a medical professional to have an evaluation. This test will include filling out several forms and hearing and vision screening. There are no blood or other lab tests that will diagnose this disorder.

While some evidence points to genetics that contribute to having ADHD, the science behind what causes it is not definitive.

Treatments

Many women with ADHD do not realize they have it. However, once you get tested and diagnosed, there are many treatments you can focus on to live your best life in the most beneficial way that works with your brain.

When you are diagnosed, you will figure out what type of ADHD you have. Although we've discussed inattentive, hyperactive, and impulsivity symptoms, there are three types of ADHD. These types are:

- **Inattentive**: This type will have you having issues organizing, finishing, or paying attention to tasks and details. You also may have problems following instructions and conversations. You will get easily distracted and forget your daily routines frequently.

- **Hyperactive-Impulsive**: You will have difficulty sitting still and talking a lot for long periods. You will often feel restless and may have impulsivity issues. When you were young, you may have had the urge to climb, jump, and run constantly. If you have impulsivity issues, you'll tend to interrupt conversations, grab things, and speak over people when they are talking. You may also have more injuries and accidents than the average person.

- **Combination**: You may also have several symptoms of each type (listed above) equally present in your personality.

The tricky thing is that symptoms can change over time as well. Although you may start with hyperactivity, it can form and change presentation as you begin to work through treatment plans. It is something to keep a close eye on.

Treatments of ADHD can include a combination of medication and behavior therapy. However, treatment will depend on how acute your symptoms are. Regardless of what treatment plan you and your medical professionals come up with, you must be comfortable. It is your choice if you want to go on medication or not. Medical intervention may be necessary to help reroute your neural pathways, but you can try several treatments until you land on the one that works best.

Good treatment plans will have you monitoring your actions, thoughts, and behaviors closely. It will also include follow-ups with your therapist and making changes when needed.

Throughout this book, we'll give you some guidance and tips on how to help yourself create the right kind of plan to help manage your symptoms. One of the best ways to begin your ADHD regimen is to stay healthy.

A healthy lifestyle is vital to helping yourself. It can make having ADHD much easier. Think about how you treat your body right now. Do you put whole, healthy foods in? Do you exercise? Practicing active methods helps your body function to its highest ability regardless of any neurodiversity you might have. However, when you eat whole foods that are clean and exercise at least five hours a week, you will be releasing beneficial chemicals into your body that will work with your ADHD in the best way possible.

<u>**Some quick tips are:**</u>

- **Develop Healthy Eating Habits**: If your eating habits are less than stellar, take small steps to improve what you are putting into your body. The better the food that goes in, the better your brain functions. Don't overwhelm yourself by doing everything all at once, though. If you've just been diagnosed with ADHD, take small steps every day to improve your lifestyle. Developing healthy eating is a lifestyle change. You won't be doing "diets." This step isn't to lose weight, it is to help your body function at its highest capacity.

- **Get at Least 3-5 Hours of Physical Activity a Week In**: Find exercises that you like and want to do. Staying physically active at least three to five days a week, one hour each day, is a fantastic way to burn ADHD energy, which will release good chemicals like endorphins and cortisol into your system. The more activity your brain gets, the more your brain can work with you, not against you.

- **Limit Your Screen Time**: This tip might be a little more tricky, especially if you work in a job with a computer, but make sure to take short breaks every hour to give your mind and body a rest from the screen. If you are home, keep a timer on your phone to remind yourself of when to put it down for a bit or get into the habit of plugging your phone in (even if it is a little bit away from you) at bedtime so you won't be tempted to check out the latest social media post or article from your favorite news outlet.

- **Sleep Is Very Important**: Different age groups need different amounts of sleep. However, recent studies have found that sleep gives your mind and body time to rest. It cleans out the toxins from your brain as well. There are several genes in the cerebral cortex and other areas of your brain that change their expression level between waking and sleeping. During these times, molecular mechanisms begin to sweep away "dirt" and replenish your mind with newer, cleaner chemicals like adenosine, GABA, melatonin, and more.

These tips are just a few blanketed ideas to get your mind working and thinking about new ways to incorporate healthy habits into your world. Throughout this book, you will find more detailed breakdowns of how to live a healthier lifestyle, the benefits of physical activity, limiting screen time, and getting enough sleep.

Conclusion

ADHD is a cognitive disorder where the neurodevelopmental status of your brain does not develop in the way a person without ADHD does. Many women live with ADHD that remains undiagnosed. You may already have developed some unhealthy coping strategies, but now more than ever, it is time to turn those maladaptive skills into restorative treatments.

Start by getting a formal diagnosis and work with a counselor you trust to build a treatment plan. If you are uncomfortable with going on medication right away, let your doctor know. You will have to try a few avenues before finding everything that works for your symptoms and your life.

However, once you start on the journey, it's much easier to shift to something new. Be an advocate for your ADHD. Be an advocate for yourself.

CHAPTER TWO

Women & ADHD

A strong woman understands that the gifts such as logic, decisiveness, and strength are just as feminine as intuition and emotional connection. She values and uses all of her gifts.
~ Nancy Rathburn

Introduction

If you believe you have ADHD or have just been diagnosed with ADHD and are an adult woman, you may think, "How was this overlooked?"

You are not alone.

The internet is rife with Reddit boards and Youtube videos of women sharing their experiences from daily life and their ADHD diagnosis shock. According to Shishira Sreenivas, a journalist on medical issues, *"Most women with ADHD get an accurate diagnosis in their late 30s or early 40s."* There are reasons for this, but that doesn't conclude having ADHD is any easier to absorb.

When you receive your diagnosis, you may feel as though the floodgates opened up and that it was the answer you've been waiting for all along, or you may feel as though you were robbed of some good years getting a jump on ADHD. There is no right or wrong way to feel. ADHD is a powerful disorder that can bring chaos into your life and give you a roadmap on how to work with your brain rather than have your brain work against you.

Why Didn't Anyone Know?

Often, ADHD symptoms in girls come out much differently than they do in the shouting, yelling, climbing, or disruptive boy. Now, it looks like there is a scientific theory that goes along with this stereotype. Researchers at the National Libraries of Medicine (NIH) conducted a study on "Females with ADHD" and developed a theory called "the female protective effect,"This theory surmises that women (and girls) have a higher threshold of external stimuli for their ADHD to come out.

Unfortunately, when external stimuli become high enough for a woman to begin experiencing ADHD symptoms, there is an opportunity to misdiagnose. Many women with ADHD symptoms get diagnosed as depressed, anxious, or more.

The "Females with ADHD" study suggests that:

> This approach based upon expert consensus will inform effective identification, treatment, and support of girls and women with ADHD. It is important to move away from the prevalent perspective that ADHD is a behavioral disorder and attend to the more subtle and/or internalized presentation that is common in females.

> It is essential to adopt a lifespan model of care to support the complex transitions experienced by females that occur in parallel to changes in clinical presentation and social circumstances.

> Treatment with pharmacological and psychological interventions is expected to impact productivity positively, decrease resource utilization, and, most importantly, improve long-term outcomes for girls and women.

This study suggests that even the DSM-V moves away from the current perspective of ADHD being a behavioral disorder. The evidence found that women with ADHD have more internalized symptoms that play out in subtle ways. The researchers explain that adopting a new model for ADHD will help improve the lives of the 3.2% of females who go undiagnosed until their 30's.

ADHD is routinely dismissed in women due to a myriad of reasons not limited to, but including:

- Role expectations (gender roles where women are "quiet" and men are the "voice).

- Comorbidities (having more than one neurological/psychological disorder).

- Hormonal fluctuations.

- Internalized symptoms (meaning your mind races instead of being outwardly hyperactive.

A Little ADHD History

While the information states *"little research explores the specific effects of ADHD on adult women,"* it doesn't make it less true and sad.

Gender bias can be unintentional, but it adds to the strain of finding out the right diagnosis for your symptoms. Since girls are less likely to be hyperactive or impulsive, their ADHD traits go unnoticed.

Dr. Stephanie Sarkis, an expert on ADHD and a psychologist, explains that women are taught to be quieter by society as girls. She points to this bias being one of the reasons that females are diagnosed later in life. The issues arise when ADHD goes undiagnosed, which leads to more problems in adult life. These problems can seriously hinder your overall life quality.

Even though ADHD research has only recently delved into ADHD in women, scientists are beginning to understand it better. Some of the myths that go along with ADHD are below:

1. ADHD is a disorder that affects only males. The beginning research studied the behavior of white, hyperactive males, which helped shape the diagnostic criteria. Unfortunately, these assessment scales are still in use today, though they are changing.

2. ADHD is a disorder for children. Although ADHD was classified (long ago) as a childhood disorder (or a Disruptive Behavior Disorder of Childhood), recent

studies show that ADHD does not simply go away at the onset of puberty. Inattentive symptoms last longer than those of hyperactivity.

Western society believes that women have a set role in their households. This act usually includes self-management, family management, household management, and career management. Each one of the tasks is controlled by executive functions that should be formed in early childhood, but are not because of ADHD.

ADHD wires a woman differently and makes the demands of daily life very difficult for them. These women, maybe even you, may turn to shame and self-blame that will downplay accomplishments and interplay with societal expectations and the executive dysfunction of ADHD. Self-worth should not be considered a viable skill, but it becomes intermixed as ADHD continues undiagnosed.

Signs & Symptoms

ADHD symptoms in women and girls are often explained away as personality traits rather than focusing on what they really are. A forgetful or chatty girl may be described as "spacey." When this girl grows into a woman, she may reach out for help and become diagnosed with anxiety or depression instead.

Awareness of ADHD and women is rising, so now more women (and hopefully girls) will start to get the help they need sooner.

Until then, know that women with ADHD face the same exhausting and overwhelming feelings as men. These emotions can include inadequate feelings, chronic stress, low self-esteem, and psychological distress. It has been noted that women with ADHD frequently feel that their lives are chaotic and out of control, and routine tasks may seem impossible or too big to tackle.

Since our culture tends to attach a "caregiver" tag to women, when things begin to feel out of control, asking her to take care of other people may make her feel as though she is drowning. These expectations people put on her can exacerbate her bad feelings.

Some signs and symptoms that you have ADHD can be:

- Time management difficulty (always showing up late to places).

- An inability to get organized.

- Constant overwhelming feelings.

- Have a history of depression and anxiety.

- Have money management issues.

There are times when ADHD has already been diagnosed in the family through a brother or sister. However, many times, women will not be diagnosed with ADHD until one of their children are first. Women with ADHD may also have other issues like insomnia, compulsive eating, or alcoholism.

Hypersensitivity is another symptom that women may have, part of their "internalized" traits. You may notice that you suffer from sensory overload often, which entails being touched by someone or even irritated by clothing materials. Your hypersensitivity can even roll over to loud sounds, strong smells, and light exposure.

Other sensitivities may leave you with physical complaints such as headaches or migraines, nausea, or stomach aches.

By the time a woman reaches her 30's or 40's and has undiagnosed ADHD, they are more than likely to have more than one other type of comorbid disorder (more than one psychological disorder). These additional disorders can complicate ADHD in entirely new ways that you will have to work with to keep your brain functioning at its highest capacity.

Some comorbidities you may be diagnosed with are:

- Anxiety

- Eating disorders (overeating or bulimia)

- Mood disorders

- Oppositional Defiant Disorder (ODD)

- Personality disorders (like Borderline personality disorder, BPD)

As we already gave you the standard version of ADHD types and their symptoms, see how women wear these symptoms differently.

Impulsive-Type in Women with ADHD:

- Have atypical behaviors (according to gender stereotypes)—including being demanding, controlling, or irritable.

- Enjoy high-risk behaviors like speeding in cars and extreme sports.

- Have addictive behaviors that can lead to abusing substances or gambling.

- Can act on negative feelings like self-harm such as cutting and picking at skin.

Inattentive-Type in Women with ADHD:

- Internalization of symptoms or never really showing their "true" selves.

- Cannot seem to pay attention to details, will make careless mistakes at work or with activities.

- Have trouble paying attention for a sustained period during any tasks.

- Won't complete daily or new duties because they get side-tracked or lose focus.

- Cannot seem to organize activities or tasks.

- Find distractions everywhere.

- Forgets to do daily activities.

- Frequently loses things. (One ADHD blogger actually writes about how often she leaves her phone in the refrigerator.)

Although all of these items seem as though they are fodder for recognizing ADHD symptoms, the challenges present are subtler symptoms that are less disruptive, women learn to camouflage their symptoms, and rating scales are skewed toward male behaviors.

If ADHD is not diagnosed and goes unfettered, there could even be a hormonal impact on women. Estrogen levels fluctuate in every woman throughout each month. They also change throughout a woman's lifespan. These fluctuations will impact the significance of ADHD symptoms. As ovarian hormones interact with each system in a woman's body, the brain is a target organ for releasing estrogen. These hormones are crucial elements that help a woman with social, emotional, and physical health. In a non-ADHD brain, estrogen protects the neurotransmitter activity that creates stabilized attention, executive functioning, concentration, motivation, and verbal memory.

Because of hormonal functions and the neurodevelopment of an ADHD brain, symptoms will decrease as estrogen wanes in the body. Estrogen decreases during each woman's hormonal cycle after ovulating, in the middle of their cycle, and near menstruation. The combination of high progesterone and low estrogen means that symptoms can vary from day-to-day living. This daily variation is called micro-fluctuation and increases a woman's sensitivity to ADHD.

As estrogen is released during puberty, ADHD symptoms can be seen more. However, the changes in hormones will appear (outwardly) more like emotional distress and anxiety. These bursts can lead to a misdiagnosis of a mood disorder, which leaves the struggling adolescent with improper treatment.

Daily Life

Between hormonal variations and untreated ADHD symptoms, women with ADHD tend to have lower self-esteem. They seem to have more psychological and emotional distress compared to their male counterparts.

Many women do not understand that their symptoms are, in fact, symptoms, and instead of finding solutions to the problem, they will try to cover them up. Women are masters of camouflaging their "less desirable traits" due to fear and shame. Others may just feel as though they live in chaos and there is nothing they can do about it.

Both of these maladaptive strategies can affect the entire family because women are usually charged with taking care of their children and the home. These less than favorable methods can also wear your daily life down, which can exacerbate your struggles.

For example, keeping up with your house, kids, job, family, and friends may be too difficult for you, and things will fall to the wayside (usually, your social life will lag behind everything else). You may always feel like you cannot "catch up," which can aggravate exhaustion and lead to chronic stress.

ADHD in your home and daily life can seem as though you are spending each day responding to requests or putting out fires. These struggles may interfere with accomplishing your goals, which can be frustrating and sad as it limits you from reaching your full potential even though you know you are smart and can do so much more.

Other daily battles can be in your home and at work.

You can gather up paper clutter until it feels as though you are drowning in forms, bills, applications, etc. Paper can gather on your desk, in your car, in your purse, and on your shelves at home. You may have a sense of impending doom like you forgot to pay bills or that something important needs fixed in your home. You can't seem to get organized and can't find important projects under all the paper.

Bills tend to be paid late, and you cannot seem to stay on budget. There is a huge possibility of overspending. Spending money you don't have or paying far too much for something is a way for you to compensate for other problems you cannot control. Instead of washing your clothes, you'll go buy new ones. If you forget a friend's birthday, you'll buy something expensive to "show how much you care," and to ease the guilt you are feeling. The instant gratification of shopping trips is only to feel regret when you get credit card bills.

Although you are determined to get organized, it doesn't seem as though you can, so you buy organizational tools, research the best tips, and spend a lot of time learning how to do it, but then never follow through with the organization. Your home may be disorganized to the point where you're embarrassed to have anyone visit, so you just stop inviting them over.

When it's time to make a decision, you may have difficulty choosing something. Many have noted that going to the grocery store is overwhelming, and they have uncertainty about what to buy. There are usually things that you forget as well, especially key ingredients for meals. Where the average person spends forty-five minutes in the store, it can take you much longer.

Finding time to relax or actually relax can be difficult as well for you. You may be unable to settle your mind. Little irritations around the house, such as the noise of a screen from another room or the children fighting in the distance, can push you over the edge, and you can become emotional instead.

Romantic relationships can be difficult because although you can care very much, it can be hard for you to show up on time for dates, remember birthdays, or just do something sweet for your partner. This strain can leave you feeling that you are not a good friend or partner.

Office jobs often feel too difficult for you to be at. The external noise and people milling around make it hard for you to complete your work. You may decide to stay late or come to work early just to get work done effectively.

Your desk is probably piled with papers; even when you clear it away, you can only seem to keep your desk clean for a day or so.

Your social life can be a bit of a mixed bag. When you were young, you may have been categorized as a tomboy because you were always busy and had a ton of energy. However, as you grew into an adult, so did social relationships. They became more complicated, and you never seemed to know when to talk or when to listen. You might have been told that you talk more than anyone else they know—but at the same time cannot keep focused on conversations, especially at parties or social gatherings, because of your ADHD mind.

The Social Deficits of Women With ADHD

Studies have shown that women with ADHD struggle more with socialization than men with ADHD.

The demands of social or emotional relationships tend to overwhelm you, and perhaps you have very few meaningful ones to avoid disappointing people. You may steer clear of making new friendships and have trouble maintaining old ones. You may find that isolation is better than the confusion and discomfort of making social mistakes or hurting another person's feelings—however lonely you may be.

Rejection is another place where emotions can increase. Your sensitivity to rejection, whether it is perceived or real, can make interactions a source of potential pain. Rather than feeling the intense emotional pain of possible rejection, avoiding many things, sometimes even trying new things, can make you feel more comfortable.

One of the most common traits that elicit shame from women with ADHD is an open sexual nature. Sexual behaviors may lean on the side of risky due to the early recognition that sex equals social acceptance. Chances are you have already taken part in risky sexual behavior or have thought about it often. You may have also had younger initiation into intercourse and other sexual activity, more casual sex, more sexual partners, and less protected sex with more transmissible sexual infections. You may have even had more unplanned pregnancies because of unsafe sexual practices.

Conclusion

Does any of this sound like you?

If you are feeling relief because your "out of the ordinary" behaviors might be symptoms of ADHD, you are not alone. ADHD behaviors come from a real place. They don't make you who you are, but they are a manageable part of how your brain works.

To be aware of ADHD (and other comorbidities that may come with it) means that you have a map of how to get to the place you want to go. The fantastic thing is that you get to decide how you want to get there. No one particularly likes taking medicine, but if you choose not to do a medical intervention at first, you will have plenty of tools to help situate your ADHD. If you choose medicine, your journey through your ADHD symptoms may be easier to maneuver through.

But you are the captain here.

Once you have ideas on how you would like to start your ADHD treatment plan, you get to take back your life. ADHD does not have to be the master of who you are.

In the next chapter, we are going to offer you some insight into executive functions and connect you to some strategies that can help you get started.

CHAPTER THREE

Executive Function & ADHD

Be strong enough to stand alone, smart enough to know when you need help, and brave enough to ask for it.
~ Ziad K. Abdelnour

Introduction

To find healthy coping strategies, techniques, and tips that will help you manage your ADHD, you should understand what executive function is. Understanding this will help you get a better idea of how your brain works, which can give you an advantage when you are looking to find helpful ways to reorganize your life.

Executive function is a set of cognitive processes and mental skills that will help you plan, monitor, and execute your goals. These functions include attentional control, inhibition, problem solving, and working memory. Many of these processes are believed to begin in your prefrontal cortex.

These operations work from the top-down and develop in childhood to eventually be automatic or instinctual. Your executive functions include three core elements, which are inhibition (including interference control and self-control), working memory, and cognitive flexibility (when your mind can shift from one topic to the next easily and flexibly). These core processes help you consider what to do next, problem solve, and plan out how to accomplish goals.

Executive function is essential for your mental and physical health and in tasks like school success, and life success. It is also vital for your cognitive, psychological, and social development.

So, what does this have to do with ADHD and you?

Executive function will help you plan, focus on projects, pay attention to conversations, remember details, follow instructions, and multi-task.

90% of people with ADHD have executive functioning problems, which are tagged with the label "executive dysfunction." Executive dysfunction impairs your ability to plan, focus on projects, pay attention to conversations, remember details, follow instructions, and multi-task.

How Does Executive Function Develop?

Executive function abilities don't develop all at once. There is a sequence to the growth of their skills as they are built one on top of another. Each executive function will interact with the next and help you regulate your behavior for positive outcomes in the future. At the same time, they start to develop by age two and be fully developed by age thirty. Those who have ADHD will have a 30-40% delay in their development time. Because of the developmental delay, as you were growing up, you may have acted on short-term goals rather than worked toward long-term ones.

The front part of your brain (prefrontal cortex) will help you find success and social effectiveness. The back part of your brain is where your learned executive function skills are stored. There are four circuits that your prefrontal cortex holds to deploy certain executive functioning skills.

These four circuits are what, when, why, and how.

The "what" circuit manages your working memory. This management helps you set goals, execute plans, and formulate steps to complete a project. The "when" circuit will guide your organizational skills and keep your timelines in check. Your "why" circuit handles your emotions, which is what you think about and how you feel. The "how" circuit guides your self-awareness of feelings and experiences.

When your executive function skills are not fully developed (or are delayed) by ADHD, it will exacerbate the ADHD symptoms such as emotional regulation, memory, and planning.

Executive Function and ADHD

ADHD is a neurodevelopmental disorder that is biologically based. This disorder impairs the function and self-management of your brain. Since executive functions are stored in your mind, there tend to be some crossover issues.

Russell Barkley, Ph.D., has been at the forefront of exploring the relationship between executive dysfunction and ADHD. He says, *"It is not that the individual does not know what to do. It is that somehow it does not get done."*

Evidence gathered from recent studies shows how ADHD affects different parts of your brain, which results in latent effects on certain executive functions. If your cerebellum is distressed, you may have issues getting to any place on time. If ADHD touches your striatum, your working memory may be off.

In these studies, scientists have linked all brain areas through a neural network (where neurons communicate via nodes). This network helps our brains absorb and process data.

Areas of your brain that connect executive function include:

- **Basil ganglia:** Responsible for motor control of your body.

- **Cerebellum:** Leads the psychical movements of your body.

- **Parietal cortex:** The back, the upper portion of your brain.

- **Prefrontal cortex:** Found in the front lobe of your brain.

- **Thalamus:** Sends sensory and motor signals to your brain.

Executive function issues can come from genetics, injuries, or damage to these brain areas. Each operation is associated with its white matter connections—the neurotransmitter system. Since your brain is made up of networking regions, any trauma or harm that comes to one part of your brain can impact all aspects of your body, including executive functioning.

Managing Executive Function and ADHD Issues

The goal of managing both ADHD and executive function boils down to the same thing: strengthening your ability to work out problems. There is no one way to do this. The process is personalized to each individual because many deficiencies can occur in the brain. The first thing to work out is to find where your dysfunctions occur. Once you find that out, you'll know the areas that will require the most work.

The National Center for Learning Disabilities (NCLD) gives some suggestions to help build stronger executive function skills.

- Break down any tasks into something smaller with a step-by-step approach.

- Use organizing tools like planners, computer calendars, watches, timers, and apps.

- Use visual aids like flow charts to review project milestones. Review these every day (or many times a day).

- Ask for verbal and written directions so you can catch all the details.

- Schedule transition periods into your daily routine to shift from one activity to another.

Getting help from outside sources, such as a therapist, can guide you in the right direction. Cognitive-behavioral Therapy (CBT) is strongly recommended to anyone who has ADHD. When using CBT, your counselor can help you find environmental triggers that spur anxiety and worsen symptoms. Occupational therapy can also help improve your motor skills, change brain patterns, and regulate your emotions.

Conclusion

Executive function is a beast. It plays such a large part in daily lives and everyday choices that you will have issues regardless of your status with ADHD without proper neural communication.

However, being diagnosed with ADHD does make it harder to unravel all the executive function problems you might have, but that doesn't mean you can't do it. Although it may seem overwhelming at first, your symptoms can guide you to where your biggest executive function challenges are. When you iron out the kinks with those, you'll be able to develop an amazing plan to start managing your brain better.

In the next chapter, we dig deeper into emotional regulation and rejection sensitivity.

CHAPTER FOUR

Emotional Regulation & Rejection Sensitivity

"She was powerful not because she wasn't scared but because she went on so strongly, despite the fear."
~Atticus

Introduction

Although having ADHD is a large enough brain issue all on its own, ADHD does not come without other complications.

As mentioned in the previous chapter, certain comorbidities can develop simply from genetics or brain chemistry. However, others come from living with ADHD and not setting the proper coping skills throughout childhood and adolescence.

Emotional regulation and rejection sensitivity go hand in hand. The more you have felt rejected as a child, whether it has happened or if you perceived the rejection, the less you can regulate your emotions. The next section will describe Rejection Sensitivity Dysphoria (RSD) and how it connects to you as a woman with ADHD and how your feelings may erupt when you feel attacked.

If you have issues with emotional regulation, we hope that by reading this information, you will find relief and know that you are affected not because of your personality, but by the way your brain developed. Understand that RSD can be managed by introducing healthy coping mechanisms into your daily life.

This disorder is extremely common for adults, even those without ADHD. You are not alone in this battle, but you can take control and not allow it to rule your life anymore.

You are strong and can build up the resistance you need to win the battle with RSD.

What is Rejection Sensitivity?

Rejection sensitivity is a common disruptive manifestation of emotional dysregulation. Women with ADHD, especially those who were not diagnosed with the disorder until adulthood, have formed this symptom throughout the years out of fear of rejection. Being sensitive to rejection becomes a dysphoric disorder that becomes traumatic for those who have it.

Although RSD is not caused by a trauma in the person's life, those with ADHD have described it as an open wound when they encounter rejection, either real or perceived. Those who have ADHD and RSD develop this disorder because they never found healthy or effective ways to cope with ADHD symptoms or the pain of rejection.

Rejection-sensitive Dysphoria can be triggered by the rejection of approval, love, respect, teasing, criticism (even if constructive), and ruminating self-criticism or negative self-talk prompted by possible or real failure. This dysphoria will quickly flip a woman's mood and match the perspective of failure. Because of the instant emotional switch when triggered, RSD can be mistaken for a full major mood disorder, including suicidal thoughts, especially with continued internalization.

When these feelings are released externally, rage becomes the first emotion the woman expresses—this rage tends to be directed at the situation or person they perceive has wounded them.

Just as quickly as the anger showed up, it could go away. A woman with ADHD can have several episodes of RSD in one day.

Many people diagnosed with RSD believe the sensitivity has always been present. However, there is also agreement that their feelings grew significantly during adolescence.

External Symptoms

When you cannot internalize RSD symptoms, which is part of the issue, you will begin to express your emotions externally. Those who suffer from RSD can exhibit behaviors like:

- Emotional outbursts that seem out of the blue.

- A withdrawal from social environments.

- Thoughts of self-harm and negative self-talk

- Avoid any setting where you may receive criticism or have the opportunity to fail at something, which is why RSD can be mixed up with social anxiety disorder.

- Have a poor reflection of self and low self-esteem.

- Become your own worst enemy with harsh self-talk that is untrue.

- Rumination on past mistakes and the preservation of memories, even if they are skewed to remember the worst parts of each incident.

- Have problems in all relationships. You may constantly feel attacked and respond defensively.

Feelings of RSD

While no one enjoys the feeling of rejection, failure, or criticism, those who have RSD find it unbearable and have extreme reactions, which is where it differs from a normal, emotional, neurotypical response of having the experience be a growth and learning moment.

Patients experiencing RSD describe their feelings as "awful," "catastrophic," "devastating," or "terrible." However, they find it hard to verbalize the pain of RSD completely, and the quality of each experience is often beyond explanation. This pain has been characterized as a physical wound, and can be seen grimacing, hunching over, and clutching their chest during their descriptions of RSD experiences.

Rejection Sensitivity Dysphoria and ADHD

The DSM-V does not include RSD as one of the symptoms of ADHD. The United States does not recognize it as a formal manifestation. However, emotional dysregulation is recognized as one of the six elements used to diagnose ADHD in the European Union.

The signs and description of ADHD in the DSM-V adhere to elementary children between six and twelve. The DSM-V has not validated ADHD in those who are sixteen years or older. The traditional criteria for diagnosis intentionally avoid the emotional, thinking, relationships, and sleeping features of ADHD because these symptoms are difficult to quantify. Those who work closely with ADHD patients observe behaviors and initiate these ideas through their network of clinicians. The signs of RSD have been noted enough throughout the years to make it an informal footnote of ADHD. Because the DSM-V does not consider other factors and uses the long history of how an ADHD nervous system works in adolescents and adults, the criteria are basically useless to anyone who works with the age range over twelve years old.

Although ADHD was first reported in the mid-1800s, RSD wasn't noted until Dr. Paul Wender, a psychologist who spent four decades dedicating his time and studies to pioneering ADHD in the 1960's. Dr. Wender was the first person to officially recognize emotional dysregulation as a highly impairing element of ADHD (previously called Hyperkinetic Impulse Disorder). Since his connection with ADHD, Wender's concept has gained new exposure and research in clinical settings.

Most recently, Dr. Fred Reimherr's founding concepts of ADHD being divided into two types: inattentive and emotional dysregulation, has begun to see the light again. Dr. Reimherr is one of the founding developers of ADHD and is credited with creating the current childhood criteria along with Wender.

This change in thinking gives ADHD a new layer of complexity, but adds defining features that can help intervene with emotional dysregulation. However, when this new wave of thought first reemerged roughly five years ago, the reception was torn. Family members of those who had ADHD were enthusiastic about the discovery as they could see how much of RSD signs were in their loved ones. Clinicians were not quite as excited because they could not connect ADHD with emotionality. They could not discover the historical basis, which had little medical publication due to the belief that RSD could not be quantified by the DSM-V.

Because RSD has now started to gain relevance among the medical community when coupled with ADHD, the obstacles are beginning to fall to the wayside. In its place, using medication and behavioral therapy offers some relief from the pain and disruption RSD causes within the lives of adults living with ADHD.

Although there has been steady research and short-term evidence that provides insight on how RSD and ADHD can be tightly interwoven, there may never be a formal criteria for the connection of RSD (or emotional dysregulation—ED) and ADHD. These reasons are as follows:

1. ED/RSD is not always present. It comes from triggered experiences.

2. Those with ED/RSD tend to be embarrassed about their over-reactions. This shame causes the patient to hide their unstable emotions and save themselves from future embarrassment.

3. Even if ED/RSD is present, there is no way to measure the symptom. If there is no way to quantify an issue, it cannot be published or discussed in research.

Although a formal write-up may never be in the DSM-V, RSD has taken an unofficial place in the United States and in the EU, so it can be treated and maintained with healthy strategies. RSD no longer has to be a debilitating or self-harming disorder that stunts your life.

Rejection Sensitivity, ADHD, & Gender

Women have a lot of pressure on them to bend to the needs of others. This pressure comes from a societal view that women should "have it all." Girls with ADHD can be seen succumbing to this viewpoint early in life. As they are often ostracized and bullied for being easily confused, disoriented by social cues, and showing too much emotion. Their inability to connect to other's feelings makes them hard wired to go against the demands society places on them. Through this rejection, RSD and anxiety develop quickly.

The brain adapts to extreme situations in extreme ways—even if that means compromising functionality in other places. Women with ADHD may have experienced a host of negative feedback in their youths. There could have been numerous episodes of bullying, exclusion, harsh punishments, and humiliation from every avenue in their lives including family members and teachers.

Eventually, their resilience has been chipped away by so much trauma that the unpredictable, repetitive experiences are repeated without realistic justification. The messages girls received about their personality, how they behaved, and what differences they excuse will create damaging messages for normal brain development and will alter the chemistry of their brain.

For many women, their RSD is histrionic. The threat of repeated rejection will trigger primitive survival mechanisms that will increase adrenaline and cortisol when placed in a potential situation of failure or rejection. You may automatically go into a fight or flight mode, setting a precedent for future social misfortune.

By the time girls with untreated (or treated) ADHD reach womanhood, they may have had decades of rejection. This experience has led them to feel like imposters in their lives. They may fear that failures will be discovered, which will open the door to another onslaught of rejection. Studies have well-documented the gender differences between lower self-esteem, less confidence, and higher anxiety regarding rejection and failure in men with ADHD, even in women without ADHD.

With this in mind, you may already be primed to expect criticism but will internalize your fear and anxiety-induced reactions to failure and rejection. The difference is that men will externalize their anxiety by using anger, blame, or defensiveness. Research has found that those who externalize angry responses will have lower stress in future experiences.

The internalization of rejection is that women begin to judge themselves based on how often they fail. This viewpoint can give them the idea that they continually disappoint everyone in their lives and become devastated by the self-fulfilling prophecy set forth by their brain chemistry. Their emotions may explode out many times a day whenever triggered.

These reactions could be seen as an overly emotional melodrama that will continue to invalidate their feeling of failure.

Some women may succumb to the idea that they are worthless and unworthy of living a good life, which is far from the truth; everyone deserves to live their best life. However, due to the chemistry of RSD, they can fall into the belief that they deserve the rejection. These unhealthy beliefs can lead to eating disorders, self-harm, substance abuse, and suicidal tendencies.

Avoiding Social Situations

Instead of dealing with rejection, women will begin to avoid any situation where there could be the potential for rejection. These women tend to be undiagnosed with ADHD, RSD, or both. They have shattered self-esteem, rageful outbursts, panic in public, or public crying. These moments will lead them to judge themselves through the harshest lens possible.

Since they will feel shame at their inability to control these impulsive reactions, some women will turn to people-pleasing. This trait will have them censoring their opinions to fit the group dynamic where they will fly under the radar. Other characteristics can develop as well. Women who cater to others will apologize for any behavior that may seem "extreme," (usually getting confused responses from others who aren't sure why apologies are needed). Some women will take the people-pleasing persona to the next level by becoming rigid perfectionists to hide their volatile nature.

These hypervigilant self-monitoring defenses will encourage emotional exhaustion and unstoppable anxiety, the opposite of what they are trying to accomplish.

When a woman chooses to avoid situations where rejection could happen, they may find that in doing so, their anxiety decreases, which seems to be the better choice than suffering through social pressure.

Isolating yourself is a choice no person should feel they have to make. Although you may feel protected in solitude, you prevent the world from hearing, seeing, and knowing the incredible woman you are. (Yes, I am talking to you!)

These powerful reactions don't have to do with your personality. Instead, they are part of a chemical make-up that can be managed and eventually rerouted in your brain if you want it to be.

Don't put or keep yourself in seclusion. This action will wreak havoc on all personal relationships. You don't have to feel shame or despair over your emotions. You are not alone with this issue. You can accept that they are not who you are, just something happening to you. You can learn how to help yourself with behavioral and cognitive therapy or medical intervention (if you are comfortable with the idea of medicine). You are an effective member of society whose brain works differently than others, so don't allow shame to envelop you and keep you from the world. Instead, take action and learn how to change the script you've been telling yourself for years.

RSD Is Not a Mood Disorder

RSD can be defined as an intense, short-lived emotional pain triggered by a distinct event of real or perceived rejection, criticism, or teasing.

Mood disorders have several characteristics such as:

- Untriggered mood changes that are out of the blue.

- Moods that are separate from what is happening in a person's life.

- Mood shifts that are gradual over weeks.

- Duration of episodes lasting two weeks or more.

For context, RSD mood characteristics are as follows:

- Mood transitions are instantaneous.

- The mood will match the trigger perception.

- An explosion of mood will last a matter of hours.

While the symptoms of RSD and ADHD are similar, symptoms and reactions of RSD and mood disorders are the opposite. As such, they will also be treated differently.

How to Treat RSD

Once you are diagnosed with RSD, you have few options to help regulate it. Medications for ADHD like guanfacine and clonidine (FDA-approved medications) have been able to have a significant effect on the symptoms of RSD. Evidence has shown that sixty percent of adults and adolescents diagnosed with RSD have found relief from their explosive episodes. Many scientists and researchers lean toward the idea that RSD is more chemical and neurological than behavioral. However, behavioral therapy and building healthy skills in this area can also deter the larger part of the episode.

Some of the most helpful tools people have noted are:

1) Knowing that they are not alone and other people have the same outbursts and reactions.

2) Learning to be kinder to themselves and releasing the shame of it.

3) Knowing that RSD is real and happens for an actual reason.

4) Understand that it will be over once the episode runs its course.

5) Finding something else to distract them from the focus of the outburst. (This skill works especially well with those who have ADHD.)

However, how you decide to work with your RSD is ultimately up to you and what you are comfortable with. Although it may seem like it is taking the easy way out, one of the best and most recommended treatments will be medication. This regime has had patients describe the relief they feel as they "put on an emotional shield," which helps them manage their moods better.

Adding cognitive and behavior therapy to the mix can strengthen your coping skills and help you understand your brain better. Therapy can help you find your triggers and identify situations that could be high-risk for those triggers. You can work with your therapist to re-evaluate your self-worth and reframe other people's opinions of who you are as a person.

Rejection sensitivity is felt by many people and does not reflect who you are, your flaws, or your downfalls. You can take the first step by accepting this idea and finding someone who will support you by pursuing treatment.

Conclusion

Rejection sensitivity dysphoria is a real and very serious issue that your brain may have. It can stop you from living your life. Instead, you may hide away from social or career opportunities where you have the chance of failing or being rejected. No one should isolate themself in that way.

If you suspect RSD hinders part of your life, talk to your counselor. You both will be able to work through a treatment plan to give yourself the life that you deserve.

The next chapter will discuss cleaning, organizing, and decluttering for the ADHD mind.

CHAPTER FIVE

Cleaning, Organizing, & Decluttering

"Life is not easy for any of us. But what of that? We must have perseverance and, above all, confidence in ourselves. We must believe we are gifted for something and that this thing must be attained."
~ Marie Curie

Introduction

One of the best-known symptoms of ADHD is that the person has trouble with organization and planning. This problem goes back to the executive function part of your brain which creates the pathways for you to keep your spaces clean and clutter-free. However, since your brain doesn't work like a neurotypical person's, your brain does not develop the skills required to keep your house organized and clear.

Instead, you may externalize your anxiety by buying things and placing them around. You may have issues with how you feel about your home, but you never seem to be able to keep it that way.

There will be days and times when you can throw yourself into the cleaning game, but since avoidance of long-sustained projects is also a symptom of ADHD, you may get bored and switch to another project that seems less daunting and way more fun.

Many women have said that they don't invite people to their house because they feel shame at their messes and clutter. Other women have said they are disappointed because they don't fall under the umbrella of what a woman is "supposed" to take care of in the house.

If you feel these things, or anything similar, it's time to flip the script. You have ADHD.

This diagnosis (or suspicion if you haven't been formally diagnosed) means that there are certain challenges in your life that you will have to accept. Once you get the fact that perhaps you aren't the best cleaner, you can put steps into your daily routine to help you clear some clutter, keep your living space organized, and get your home clean, most of the time.

The biggest thing you can do is not put pressure on yourself and your home. To say that your home will "never" be dirty again is unrealistic, even for those who do not have ADHD. Start small and do things one step at a time, and you can start to see some real change in the way your environment feels to you.

The Problem With Clutter & Organization

If you live in a place with papers strewn everywhere, dirty dishes piled in the sink, and spoiled food in your refrigerator, you're not alone. We all struggle with keeping our environments clean from time to time. However, if you have a chronic issue with cleanliness, cannot organize yourself, and find that your clutter seems to grow every day, there may be a bigger issue.

Since you are reading this book, we will assume that you have recently been diagnosed with or have long suspected that you have ADHD.

Some problems come from clutter and disorganization, especially when you have ADHD. You may lose your keys, glasses, remotes, etc., frequently. You may miss deadlines for work because you don't keep track of them and cannot find your projects because they are buried under piles of other projects.

The first thing you can do to help yourself with cleaning and clearing away big messes is to take a step back and realize you are not lazy, dirty, or a mess; it's not your fault at all. It's the way your brain develops.

It's a common symptom that many, many, many adult women with ADHD have.

Cleaning with ADHD requires an emotional and logical preparation to begin the task. Once you start, you'll have to follow through with the ideas and then complete them.

This mental stimulation is exactly the opposite of what an ADHD brain does.

Just because this type of planning works against the ADHD mind doesn't mean that you'll never live in a home that is clean and free of any kind of clutter. However unrealistic it may seem, you CAN work a cleaning routine into your daily life.

You just have to take some smaller steps first.

If you've already been diagnosed with ADHD and have gone on medication to stimulate your brain, know that this medication may help you with the task at hand. But, medication isn't the only way that you can help yourself.

First, you should identify your goal.

Do you want to improve your living space? Do you want to be able to find important objects easier? Would you like to get rid of the excess clutter in your home?

Once you decide on the most important task for you first, you'll have to make a few choices.

Should you decide that improving your living space is your biggest priority, you're going to have to find the right solution for you to get there. Katy Rollins, writer at ADDitude magazine and woman with ADHD, says:

> I decided to cut out my extracurricular activities right now, aside from cleaning and organizing my house. I don't know that I would recommend that for everyone, but it's what's working for me right now. It's given me a new perspective—I have a better understanding of exactly what it takes for me to maintain my home. I calculated that it takes twenty to twenty-five hours per week to manage and care for my household (timers can help with figuring this out).

Once Rollins developed her plan and got it down into her routine, she began delegating chores to other people (kids and partners) in her home. Her goal for her life was:

- Do one load of laundry a day.

- Make sure no dishes are in the sink (almost every day).

- Scoop cat litter daily.

That is it. Those are the chores that she repeats daily. She does this so she won't get bored with everything else. Her next steps are to "sprinkle weekly tasks into [her] week." These tasks include cleaning the bathrooms, mopping the floors, and sweeping. Another small trick she uses is to keep a sponge next to the sink in her bathroom to wipe down the counter whenever it needs it (plus, bonus, she always sees the sponge, so she never forgets to clean the counter).

Finally, Rollins admits that while her home isn't showroom clean, she is no longer embarrassed to have people over or when they may stop over suddenly. She took the organization and clutter into her hands and found a way that worked for her.

By using action, she can make sure that daily tasks are done daily and add other tasks in—like organizing her children's rooms—after her priority chores are completed. She states that her sense of inner peace and self-esteem has improved, and if she misses a day, she won't let that ruin her routine. Now, she says, she has things under better control and is inspired to do more with her house.

While Rollins' tips work for her, don't think you have to adhere to them. Find what works best for your brain and lifestyle. You may have to try several things before one process or procedure sticks. But, the point is that once you set your goal, you can keep trying until you find the right path.

Two things you can keep in mind when starting on your cleaning and organizing journey are:

1) **Make Things Easier on Yourself**: Put items back where you got them when you're done using them. Use some type of organizational hack to make things just as easy to put away as they were to get them out of their place.

2) **Get Rid of Excess Belongings**: The word "purge" can be appropriate in this situation. It's almost impossible to organize your environment if you have ADHD and lots of stuff. Do yourself a favor and think about purging each space of things you don't need.

Keep these two ideas in your mind as you figure out how to best organize your home and clear away excess clutter. However, since you may not know where to start, the next section provides you with some tips that may be helpful for you.

How to Keep Your Area Clean & Organized (Most of The Time)

You're not going to keep your home and workspace clean all the time. Admit it to yourself and accept it. Not because you won't be dedicated to the cause of cleanliness and organization, but because you are human with human distractions like sickness, birthday parties, exhaustion, etc.

Professional organizers will tell you to do "this," or "that," exactly like "this." But that will never work with your ADHD brain because your brain doesn't work the way other people do.

Expert organizers emphasize the beauty of tools over efficiency—you need to have a way for your organization to be efficient. At any given moment, an ADHD brain can become overwhelmed or underwhelmed—focusing on how pretty things look in their place and adding in an extra step or two to make it "look nice" will probably lose your interest or become overwhelmed with the idea, before you even pick up a basket.

Instead, put your attention toward what is the most efficient for your lifestyle. Keep cooking supplies (like spices, flours, rice, etc.) in original packages. Don't worry about taking cotton swabs out of their container. Don't put your medication in a drawer or cabinet. Keep it out where you can see it.

Have your organizational methods use as few steps as possible.

Find efficiency.

If You Have Clutter, it's Time to Purge Some Stuff

Look around your home. Do you see clutter?

You might not recognize that the big piles of paper stashed in the corner of your living room or the kitchen counter filled up with utensils, tchotchkes, and boxed foods are actually clutter. You might think, *"If I can see the floor, my home is clean."*

That's okay and normal for a woman with ADHD. However, just because you can see the floor doesn't mean your house is clean or that you have good cleaning habits. More than likely, it's overwhelming to really look at a room and see that those piles of paper are months or years old. The trinkets are dirty and broken, and the plant you got a few months ago has been long dead.

But, you can start on your cleaning journey by getting rid of most of the items in your house.

Knowing what to throw out and what to keep may sound overwhelming, but ask yourself this: Would taking care of a specific item in the way it was meant to be taken care of (if you have trinkets, that means cleaning them regularly or dusting them weekly; with clothes if would you want to wash, dry, iron, fold and put them away daily) be worth your time and effort.

If you answer this question with "yes," keep it. If you answer "no," you know what to do: donate it or throw it away. There are many people who may not have what you do and may need it. Always consider donating if the object is in good condition and you know it can get love and use somewhere else.

Chances are, you're going to answer "no" more often than "yes." This honesty will help you cut down on having too much clutter faster than you realize. The less you have, the less time there will be keeping it organized and clean.

Once you get rid of the clutter, make sure that you aren't purchasing new stuff to take the place of the old items. If your ADHD is impulsive, and you happen to buy things without much thought, it might be time to put alerts or alarms on your credit cards so they can tell you when you've hit a certain limit.

If you live with a partner or a roommate, having them keep you in check when buying something new is also a good idea (but you can't get mad at them when they do it).

If you would prefer not to enlist help from your housemates or family, then get in the habit of asking yourself whether you really need whatever you are buying. How will you take care of it? Where will you put it once it's in your home? What will you feel after you purchase it? Give yourself some perspective on material possessions, and you can greatly cut your spending costs.

Find Your Target Areas

You may not have to focus on throwing out clutter. First, you may want to pinpoint the target spots in your home that collect the most mess. Remember, whatever works for you is the best way that works!

Look at your home and workspace and ask yourself: *"What can I do to make things easier on myself?"* The only way to get some real work accomplished is honesty.

Firstly, what is the biggest problem area? Do you have too many shoes? Are clothes thrown everywhere? Do you have gaggles of paper piles strewn all over the place? Make a list of the problem areas from biggest to smallest and tackle one room at a time.

Secondly, choose where you want to start. You don't have to start clearing away the biggest area first, but you have to clean up one spot. Pick where you want to begin and get comfortable getting rid of your stuff. Clearing away each area can show you a new way to look at your home and its cleanliness.

Lastly, with the items you've kept, figure out how to make things easier on yourself. Find ways to make and keep the areas clutter-free.

Clothes

Do your clothes get tossed on the floor? Over a bench? Left in the bathroom?

Add hooks to your doors to hang the clothes you plan on wearing again before washing.

For example, hanging things like pajamas on a hook can alleviate the stress of having clothes build up on the floor or save you from looking for them when you are getting ready for bed.

Keep a laundry basket in these areas if you do not wear clothes a second time but they are thrown over the floor in your bathroom, laundry room, or bedroom. Take (and keep) the lid off to make it even easier.

If you have issues with throwing clothes on the floor, even after they are clean, dedicate one or two baskets to clean clothes only. Keep clean clothes in these baskets until you are ready to fold them—but still, make folding your clothes a priority in your routine.

Kitchen

What are your biggest problem areas in the kitchen? Are the counters cleaned off? Do you have coffee accessories thrown everywhere? Do fruit and spices get tossed into the same place?

To solve this problem, get baskets. Lots of baskets. (After you clear the counters and tables off, of course.)

Keep your coffee supplies in one basket. Your fruit in another. Your spices in a third, and so on. Get a basket for every item you have put away.

Give each basket of items a specific place on your counter or table (for example, keep fruit near the snack drawers or other places you have food).

Desk

Your desk at work, at home, or both can be a catalyst for clutter. Do you have papers that pile up everywhere? Can you not find the proper tools needed to complete a task?

Get yourself a few filing shelves with no lids. Keep two on your desk—one for "to-read" items and one for "read" items. Put your pencils, paperclips, rubber bands, post-it notes, etc., in baskets (just like the kitchen), and get a large calendar to add your deadlines on. Set the calendar on your desk, so it's always in view.

Trash

Where does most trash wind up? Put a garbage can close to that area. Don't hide it, don't keep a lid on it—just keep it near where garbage piles up and make it easy for yourself to throw things away instead of leaving them on the floor, table, counter, etc.

For example, if you eat snacks in front of the TV, put a can next to the couch to throw the wrappers into the garbage can as soon as you are done eating the snack.

Finishing Chores Once They Are Started

Once you start on a chore, it can be hard to finish just from the sheer boredom of the task. When you're stuck doing tedious tasks, your brain is wired to seek out more exciting prospects. If you find that this is the case for you, know that you can get organized. It will just take you a little longer than neurotypical people to discover and develop the right techniques for you.

It is crucial to find the right tools that work for you. You may even need a combination of approaches to make a new plan stick.

The key to seeing if a strategy works is to try it for a few weeks. Try to do something for three weeks in a row to see if it works for you. If you find that it doesn't work, move on to a new strategy, but if you feel like some parts of the plan are working, but something is still missing, add a new piece to the current system. The most important part is to keep trying to figure things out. If one approach doesn't work, don't give up. Instead, make a game out of it to find the right pieces to the ADHD puzzle.

Below are some tricks to test out. See if any of them, a combination of them, or none of them work for you:

1. **Build a Chore Chart**: With ADHD, chances are you forget what chores still need to be done or lose track of what has already been cleaned. Creating a chart where you organize chores by day (for example, vacuum on Thursdays), and checking them off when each is done, can help you remember to do things and save you energy on doing the same task more than once a week.

   With this chart, you can create a new one each week so that you have the projects fresh in your mind. You can also place the chart somewhere you can see it often, like in the kitchen on the refrigerator or in a room where you spend most of your time.

   A dry-erase board is fantastic if you'd like to make things easier on yourself. However, you can always purchase standard chore charts too. If you are a fan of technology, organizational apps can give you reminders, timers, and alarms. Just make sure to keep the app on your phone's home screen so you don't forget you have it.

2. **Chunk up Your Time**: Having ADHD gives you a lot of superpowers, and one of those is that you are high on energy, which means you'll clean like a speed demon and do a great job at it. When you chunk out your time, you will be cleaning things in short bursts to avoid getting bored with a task.

Place timers around your house (or use your phone). If you need to clean the kitchen, take the large task and break it into smaller ones like dishes, counters, floors, cupboards, etc.

Then clean each area throughout the day or do one task one day a week. Use the timers to keep track of how much time you spend doing the project, and try to keep the cleaning time to that amount of time.

Or, you can set the timer for fifteen to forty-five minutes and stop when the timer goes off. Knowing that a chore will end in a shorter time can make it easier to complete.

3. **Think About the Kids**: If you don't have children, you don't have to read this one if you don't want to, but if you do have kids, you have to think about what clutter and disorganization do to their living space. Children don't have to live in an immaculate home, but they do best in a predictable environment (especially if they also have ADHD).

Cleaning routines and routine cleaning purges can help them feel as though they are living in stability and that you provide that solid space for them to feel safe.

4. **Block Out Some Time**: Pick one day out of the week and one time during that day to do a chore. Block out this time to complete it. Keep in mind you'll have to do this for each chore, not only to do one chore a week. Designate this time for the assignment and follow your schedule. Using time blocks can help you get on track and give you a chance to hit each part of your home you need to clean.

5. **Box Out Your Time**: Time blocking and time boxing are similar in that you schedule a time during a specific day to clean certain parts of your living environment.

However, boxing your time means that you set a time to do a chore and set a timer.

When the timer goes off, stop that chore no matter what. These times should be up to forty-five minutes. Anything longer and you might lose interest.

6. **Do Two Things at Once**: One of the superpowers of ADHD is that you are a brilliant multi-tasker. While it is technically impossible to clean two things simultaneously, you can do other things while you clean.

You can try to listen to an audiobook, stream a show (or social media platform), pretend you are a character in a skit that has to clean, race with other people in your household to see who can get it done first, talk to a friend on the phone, and more. The options are endless with this one and can help keep your brain from wandering and getting bored.

7. **Map Out a Routine**: Certain chores have to be done weekly or daily. When you have tasks that need to be repeated frequently, you can build a habit through a routine. To start, make a list of all the chores you have. Then figure out what ones need to be completed daily and what ones should be done weekly.

If you have fourteen chores, you can do two a day. Or, you can pick one day to do the weekly chores and do three daily chores a day—the options are endless and yours. Try a few different ways to see what one works best for you.

You can also schedule the same chores for the same day of the week such as doing laundry on Saturday, sweeping the floors (with vacuum) on Thursday, etc. Having the same chores on the same day of the week every week can have you build a habit into your routine in no time (it takes a neurotypical person twenty-one days to make a habit, so that it may take a neurodivergent brain a little longer than that).

8. **Set Reminders**: You can do this one in a couple of ways. First, you can put a calendar near your cleaning supplies (as long as you can see it every day), then add each chore to a different day.

The second way is to add an alarm system to your phone calendar. This way, you will get notifications about each undertaking when scheduled and when it is time to finish this off.

9. **Use Tools Efficiently**: Cleaning supplies do not need to go in one specific

area, especially when you have ADHD. Keep cleaning supplies in the room they are meant to clean. For example, toilet bowl cleaner, glass cleaner, a sponge, a brush, and multipurpose surface cleaner can all be stored in the bathroom.

When you keep the cleaning supplies in each room, you remove the option to have to find the stores and walk somewhere else where you may get distracted. This method makes cleaning accessible and simple.

10. Give Yourself a Cookie: Once you're done with a chore, reward yourself somehow. It doesn't have to be a cookie, but it can be something that is more on track for you, your life, or your tastes.

Those with ADHD do really well with positive reinforcement. What better way to treat yourself positively than rewarding yourself for a job well done?

11. Delegate: If you have the means and cannot seem to sit down and create a proper plan of action, you can always hire a professional organizer. Make sure the organization expert understands what it means to have ADHD and give them examples of tools you'd like to try. Coming into a clean home can give you the extra motivation to keep it that way.

If you do not have the means, but have roommates or live with your family, have them join in the fun. You can dedicate certain cleaning times for everyone to do together. Having extra help can be less overwhelming, and you can make it fun too.

12. Reframe the Way You Think About Cleaning: Women with ADHD often speak badly about themselves and their abilities to keep spaces clean, negative talk about yourself can wear you down, quickly.

Instead, when an unfavorable voice crosses your mind, tell it that you can do better. Then take the adverse message and flip it to something more positive.

For example, instead of, *"I'll never get this house clean,"* you can say, *"I'll work to get this house clean."* Or change, *"I'm such a slob,"* to, *"I'm learning how to clean better."*

The more positive talk you do for yourself, the more you can start to see your accomplishments, and the more proud you will feel of yourself and your actions.

No one expects you to be perfect, and you shouldn't either. Take small steps to accomplish larger goals and soon, you'll start to see results. If you feel bored with chores, it's okay—if you put off chores, be nice to yourself.

Conclusion

Keeping a clean and organized home is completely doable for someone who has ADHD. Try out the tips and tricks in this chapter and see what works for you. You may not stick to only these examples once you get your routine rolling in a good direction, but this is a great place to start.

The next chapter will discuss women, ADHD, and their social lives.

CHAPTER SIX

ADHD & Social Life

"You must know that you can do this. You are strong. And you will make it. Just hang on and keep believing in yourself, always."
~ Heather A. Stillufsen

Introduction

Any relationship is hard. Ask anyone who has ever been in a romantic partnership or a deep friendship.

Having people in your life takes work, maintenance, and thoughtfulness. There are a lot of times when it is hard for someone with ADHD to make friends because some of their symptoms can make for unique experiences when others are not used to these traits. However, it can also be hard for you to have friends because some of the ADHD symptoms make it hard to find new friends and build lasting relationships.

Due to problems such as impulsiveness, mood regulation, hyperactivity, or attention issues, it may have been hard for you to develop healthy boundaries and social skills. Some may misread your behavior and see your inattentiveness as being shy or your impulsivity as an act of aggression.

Even without ADHD, many people don't prioritize friendships. We all get preoccupied with our lives. Cynthia Hammer, ADHD coach and MSW, explains that, *"Someone with ADHD who is also trying to manage their symptoms may find it even more challenging to get and maintain connections with others."*

Just because there are some extra challenges doesn't mean all is lost. ADHD isn't the

52

end all be all of the friend killers. In fact, it can make you an amazing friend who thinks outside of the box, can care like no one else, and shows your big heart whenever you can.

ADHD & Social Isolation

In one of the previous chapters, we discussed rejection sensitivity dysphoria (RSD). This disorder can be an aspect of ADHD, and it can cause you to isolate, even when you feel lonely socially. However, RSD isn't the only reason women with ADHD isolate themselves socially.

Dr. Michelle Novotni, the former president of the Attention Deficit Disorder Association and an internationally known expert on ADHD, discusses why it's easier for those with ADHD (women especially) to isolate rather than put themselves into uncomfortable situations socially.

Novotni discusses the difference between men and women and the double standard. Both a man and a woman can violate the same social rule. Where men will be excused for it "because he is a man," a woman won't be. This incongruence happens because women are supposed to "have better manners," and they should know more about appropriate social behaviors.

This excuse is crap.

Women and men should be held to the same standards, but in our society they are not. However, when a woman has to contend with the social impairment of ADHD, many feel they have a weakened understanding of how to be social.

Women with ADHD have similar views about where they feel exposed and vulnerable. Some of these areas are:

- No social connections with acquaintances, business associates, and friends.

- How to master multi-tasking by switching between family, home, work, and friends.

- An inability to ask for help or assert their news.

- Feeling sadness due to a lack of positive social interaction leads to isolation.

Step Out of Isolation

To avoid staying in an isolated frame of reference, you can do a few things to help yourself.

Firstly, don't be too hard on yourself. Social skills are not taught in school. We were never given a handout that had the "dos and don'ts" of what is appropriate in certain situations. However, a large part of the population believes you should just automatically know and understand the rules to sustainable relationships. You don't want to be friends with those people. Those people will often leave you feeling confused, dismissed, rejected, and lonely. You don't deserve to feel that way at all.

Instead, find people who will talk to you, give you feedback, and who see all the amazing parts of you as you are. You can ask them what social skills you need improvement on. When they tell you, listen with an open and honest mind—they aren't pointing out bad things about you. They explain social norms and cues that you may miss because of ADHD. You should also ask them about your strengths, so you can hear positive feedback to balance out the constructive criticism.

Multi-Tasking Relationships

Women do not have the luxury of focusing on one task, especially as mothers, counselors, household managers, wives and partners, career women, students, social coordinators, and more.

Although you're a master multi-tasker, being responsible for a house, family, and career can create multiple problems. Trying to organize your house is difficult enough as we've discussed in the previous chapter. When you add in children and their social calendar, schoolwork, and other aspects of their care (feeding them, making sure they are bathed, etc.), you may feel exhausted and insecure about yourself.

Being physically and emotionally drained will leave you with very little energy to put into even a single friendship. It becomes easier to shut down than to put yourself in a possibly embarrassing situation.

If you're unable to get organized or you feel like you can't catch up, find support from a therapist, counselor, or ADHD coach who can help you develop strategies and routines to help you remove (or shrink) these kinds of obstacles.

Another thing you can do is forget the adage that women should "have it all," "do it all," and, "be it all." None of us can be everything for everyone all the time, and we shouldn't be expected to. Instead, give your family tasks to do around the house. Spouses and older children can do some work with meals. They can help make dinners and pack school lunches. Younger children can pick up pet poop, fold clothes, pick stuff up off the floor, and put things away.

Asserting Yourself Even When You Hate Conflict

When there are things that we don't like, we often swallow it down, push it away, or talk ourselves into believing that we are the ones who are at fault (in some way). However, that is not always the case. Others views, opinions, actions, and words can have an effect on you, and you have every right to say, *"I don't like this."*

But, you may have a hard time doing it, which is normal and natural. If you cannot trust your friends and partner to appreciate and understand that your feelings are your own, your social relationships will not flourish.

Instead you'll have to learn to ask for what you want and speak up about things that you don't like. You can get the advice of a counselor, friend, therapist, or coach. Being assertive isn't the same thing as being aggressive. There may be a fine line for you right now because your moods may be out of whack, but with a little coaching and coaxing, you're going to be able to set your boundaries in a healthy and respectful way.

ADHD & Strong Feelings

Women are already associated with being emotional and there could be times when you've been told you're overreacting to something, when you don't understand how it is seen as a big feeling.

The thing is that the ADHD brain regulates emotions differently than the neurotypical one, so instead of having a reaction like "everyone else" you're going to react like a woman who has ADHD would.

CHAPTER SEVEN

ADHD & Friendships

Challenges

Along with the laundry list of symptoms that infringe on your daily life, ADHD affects your social life as well. Even if you don't find yourself in social isolation, maintaining healthy friendships where both friends put similar effort into the relationship can bring symptomatic challenges to amicable relationships.

Feeling Overwhelmed

Because you already have issues managing your daily tasks like finishing tasks, keeping appointments, and making deadlines, you may feel overwhelmed by having friends in your life, especially when they bring their own burdens.

Extra "life" stuff, such as when your basement floods or your washer breaks, will put added pressure on your shoulders, which will leave little attention and energy to direct toward friendships. You'll find your desire to hang out with a friend may get pushed to the back of the line, or you'll forget about them completely.

Getting Bored

Although you enjoy having friends or have a deep desire to have good friends, you might get bored with them. There may be times when you want to take a break from their company, and you find it hard to enjoy their company or pay attention to them regularly. There may be times when you even begin daydreaming about doing other things while spending time with them.

This inattentive feeling may leave you more interested in learning how to play a new video game or going to a movie by yourself instead of hanging out with your friend.

Inconsistency With Friendships

When you need to take a break from your friends, you expect them to be around when you reach back out to them. You won't see someone for many months, and while you are okay with it, other people are not. They may feel that you only contact them when you get bored or have nothing better to do. Or, they may find your behavior too fickle and erratic to be trusted.

Poor Memory

Your poor memory can add an extra layer of the challenge when you can't remember important details about your friend's life. Does your friend have children? Do you know their names? Do you have any pregnant friends? When is your friend's next birthday?

These types of personal facts are vital to the success of a friendship. People want to know and feel they have importance in your life, and if you cannot refer back to them in future conversations, they may think that you aren't interested in their life.

Being a friend means sharing important parts of your life with others and vice versa. They want to listen to your successes and failures and expect the same treatment in return. These actions let your friend know that you value them and that they value you.

If you find yourself saying, *"I don't remember,"* or *"I forgot you said that,"* they will get the impression they aren't important enough to you. Trying to correct the issue by avoiding certain topics because you can't remember essential items makes things hard to build a long-term, healthy friendship. When you cannot share memories of time spent together, you leave the impression that your company with them is not of interest to you.

Your Self-Esteem

If you have low self-esteem, it can be hard to develop friendships, especially with new people. You may not have the confidence to reach out to a new person.

Even if you want to make friends, you may believe that people wouldn't want to be around you. This type of thinking can hold you back from reaching out to connect with someone.

Your Depression & Anxiety

As a woman with ADHD, you may have other comorbidities like depression, anxiety, and mood disorders.

Depression shifts your mood downward with low energy and a lack of desire to talk to people (sometimes even leaving the house or getting out of bed is difficult as well). This condition can put a strain on a friendship if you never want to be around the person and will not accept their help.

Social anxiety disorder (SAD) can be an issue where any social interaction will leave you jumping out of your skin with stress and tension at the thought of hanging out with someone. This feeling makes it hard to put yourself in situations where other people may reject or make fun of you. Staying out of social situations makes it hard to make new friends.

Lack of Friends Equals a Lack of Acceptance

Society tells women that if they have a lot of friends, they should have self-worth. Identity is defined by how strong their relationships are. However, social interactions can add an extra layer of stress and struggles for a woman with ADHD. Since friendship is about compromise, cooperation, awareness of others' emotions, needs, and relationship maintenance, chances are you may feel low or no self-worth.

The Shame of Friendship

Women are the members of the household who are supposed to remember to send birthday cards or purchase birthday presents. If someone does something nice for her or their family, that woman is supposed to send a thank you note. They are supposed to make little gifts for their children's class and hand out gifts to teachers, make crafts for friends, and so on. All of these items are charged to the woman. But, when a woman with ADHD is the head of the household, family members, family friends, and personal friends may start to think that her long silence is her lack of interest in the relationship.

Although this is untrue, this kind of gap in the relationship leaves the woman with ADHD feeling shame because they forgot something else in their friend's life. This shame leads to future avoidance of the friend, which makes for an inevitable loss of another friendship.

Reciprocating is Difficult

Your friend does something nice for you, and you want to do something back for her, or it's your turn to host the dinner party with your group of friends. No matter what the reciprocal nature of the event is, you want to treat people as they treat you, with love, care, and kindness. But, it's not always that simple.

When you have to host a dinner party, you may "clean" the night before by throwing all your clutter into the garage. You may also be the only one allowed in your kitchen because you don't want anyone to see how disorganized or dirty your refrigerator is. Basically, you won't be able to enjoy your time with your friends because you're stressing over what your house looks like, and you're embarrassed to talk about it.

When you don't share your plights, you aren't revealing your whole self to your friends, and they deserve to get to know who you are.

Time Issues

No matter how much you plan, you're going to be late. Or, you're going to be so early that you might be ready to leave when your friend shows up.

You can set all the timers in the world when you make plans. You can have reminders, notifications, and sticky notes posted all over your home, and something can happen that will kick your distraction mode into high gear. You can lose your keys, get stuck in traffic, or find that you desperately need coffee; these situations, and many others, will mean that you are late. Sometimes you are just late. But others, you are late, late. This inconsistency can show people that their time is not important to you when really it is.

Your Phone is Your Lifeline

On the days when your ADHD is going haywire, you may be unable to put your phone down. Your brain may need extra jolts of dopamine, and what better way to get it than through the ease of clicking through an app on your phone or making an instant purchase from a place that will send you an item in two days or less.

The lack of attention to your friends may leave them a little insulted that your phone seems more interesting than what they have to say. This feeling can be a slippery slope if they don't understand how your brain works.

Your Thoughts May Not Cooperate

There may be times when your brain has a thought, and it just needs to be said right now. No matter who else is speaking or what they are saying. These are the times when the conversational part of your brain is fizzling out, and your social skill set is on the fritz. It's not that you ignore your friend, but it might seem that way. It may also come across that you're only interested in talking about yourself, your problems, and your life.

Throughout this long list of challenges, you may have found some similarities or differences in managing or handling your friendships. If you feel low about yourself, have shame about your ADHD, and are uncertain about how to help yourself step out of the negative mindset, never fear because you can get out of the cycle you're stuck in.

If you can maintain certain friendships and this part of ADHD doesn't affect your life, you might be able to pick up some helpful tips to pass on to others, your child, or even help yourself in a new way.

You deserve to have friends, and people deserve to know you. You can shine your light on your corner of the world and spread joy to whomever you want. The section below will give you some advice and tips on improving friendships to develop deep relationships that last.

You Can Improve Your Friendships

Lots of people have problems showing their vulnerable sides. However, when you have ADHD, there may be extra layers of vulnerability that you're afraid to share. You may feel as though people will not accept you for who you truly are, or you may get nervous that they won't understand your idiosyncrasies. However, if you can accept your friends for who they are and can be supportive and loving despite the challenges that come with ADHD, you owe it to yourself to let others support and love you.

If you feel like you want some help making friendships, the great news is that you can. It just takes a little shift of your mind and some reframing of your negative thoughts. You'll discover that more people accept you than you originally believed possible.

First, figure out what type of friend you are.

There are articles and anecdotes all over the internet, in books, newspapers, and more of women giving their personal experiences with ADHD friendships and the obstacles they took to overcome them. However, each ADHD subtype has different hardships to defeat.

Women with Hyperactive-Impulsive ADHD will:

- Get bored easily

- Interrupt others

- Ignore social rules

- Blurt out negative criticism

- Control the conversations

- Focus the conversation on themselves

- Enhance their stimulation level with substances

- End frustrating relationships.

Women with Inattentive ADHD will:

- Become overwhelmed by social and emotional demands

- Avoid impromptu social gatherings

- Have anxiety in unfamiliar environments (especially with a lot of people)

- Second-guess and censor their feelings and responses if they feel conflict coming

- Create flaws to have others avoid them, so they don't have to avoid others.

- Label mistakes as character flaws

- Assume everyone will reject or criticize them

Do any of these traits sound like you? Do you have ideas on how to combat them, or are you in denial that any of these items happen? Note that we all have flaws, make mistakes, and have issues we need to resolve. These traits of ADHD are not your personality. They are symptoms of a disorder. They cause struggles within your brain that you can regulate, and while there may be times when you fall back into old habits, you will be able to pick yourself back up and move forward to the next time where you will implement lessons learned and grow from the experience.

ADHD & Social Strategies

- <u>Accept who you are</u>. You cannot change what the social expectations of society are any more than you can change how your brain is wired. However, you can rewrite the narrative about ADHD and the social perspective, so you no longer give your power over them.

Right now, you may look through the lens of anxiety, depression, and the weight put on your shoulders by the world. Instead, shift your glasses to accept yourself and your exceptional needs. Once you begin to look at the world with new eyes, you can relieve yourself from self-judgment and social restraint. Then, instead of apologizing for symptoms and mistakes, you can act on your strengths.

Look at yourself with respect and value over what everyone else says, thinks, and does. When you do this, you can find confidence in yourself and sow nurturing and meaningful friendships.

- <u>Work with technology, don't let it work you</u>. We've probably made it very clear that your brain functions in a unique way. ADHD is caused by the depletion of certain chemicals that allow a brain to work in a neurotypical way. So, one way to replenish these chemicals—especially dopamine—is to seek out instant gratification.

When you are online, clicking on something and getting a reward like bonus points in a game or an instant purchase will push the right "button" in your brain and release that much-needed shot of dopamine. However, you may start to rely on the internet or that "quick fix" to get you through the day when that happens.

Instead of letting the internet and technology rule you, take power back into your own hands. Use technology, social media platforms, and apps to help organize your life to work with ADHD.

Technology can alleviate some of the stress of social connections by sending texts instead of calling. For example, sending a weekly *"You're in my thoughts"* text can keep the communication going.

Use apps and a digital calendar to remind you of get-togethers, birthdays, etc. Notifications and alarms can give you the heads up that you're needed elsewhere (and soon). If you work them right—try to set them thirty to forty-five minutes before you need to leave so you can transition into the "get out of the house mode."

- <u>Be transparent about your ADHD</u>. You have flaws. Your friends have flaws. Creating an open and honest relationship means opening up to people so they can accept all parts of who you are, and concurrently, you'll accept all parts of them as well. This action is a huge part of building a deep and lasting friendship. When you are honest about your ADHD symptoms, you're accepting that you aren't perfect (and that you are okay with it, woo!), but you are putting your trust in another person to love and care for all parts of you. And you are worth having that.

When you talk to your friends about your ADHD, there is no need to apologize. Explain it clearly while still showing their needs for attention. *"If I don't respond to your text right away, please text me again. Chances are I read it and got distracted, but I always want to respond to you. You are important to me."*

Make sure that you give your trust to the right kind of people. If you try to talk to someone but they are unwilling or unable to listen to you without making you feel bad about yourself, assess the friendship and see if it is worth your time. Other people in the world will treat you with the respect and love that you deserve.

- <u>Understand what triggers your ADHD</u>. Becoming more self-aware of your actions and what makes your brain tick will take a little vigilance. For example, some women with ADHD may want to join a committee or club because it is of interest to them, but they are wary because their symptoms may make them feel awkward or uncomfortable at one point or another. Instead of avoiding what you want to do, understand that your brain will be looking for constant stimulation—your triggers may include losing eye contact, getting bored, tuning out, changing the subject, or having a desire to interrupt conversations.

There is a fine line between respecting your brain and indulging in the trigger points. Doing so will take practice. However, if you find yourself growing bored or looking around the table wishing you were somewhere else, excuse yourself. Take a break by going to the bathroom or heading outside for a few moments. Your brain may move in different ways than other people's, but taking a break and releasing yourself may be what it needs to continue with your encounter. If resting and switching your environment for a few minutes doesn't work, give yourself permission to duck out of the event early.

- <u>Figure out your favorite way to move</u>. Plan activities with friends where you can move around. Go to the park, walk through your neighborhood, ride bikes, etc. When you have ADHD, you'll have to move at your own pace. Endeavors like shopping or hangouts for lunch might not be up your alley. You're more likely to drive your focus to your friend when you get moving since you're an excellent multi-tasker. If you are invited to a dinner or a movie with a friend, let them know that it's hard for you to sit still, but you want to go out with them. Suggest other activities that you know (or hope) you'll both enjoy.

- <u>So you want to host an event</u>. Do it! You should! Once you put your focus into something, you can make it amazing. But you're going to have to work with your ADHD to get these things done. Follow the tips below on hosting a dinner party from Dr. Elizabeth B. Littman, a pioneer of gender differences in ADHD. She is also internationally recognized as an ADHD expert and an author of ADHD books. These tips for a dinner party can be used for other events by honing a few items you're looking to plan.

- Host a gathering in warmer weather. Use the event to eat outside as a casual, buffet-style meal. It also means less clean-up!

- Have a small group of people over instead of a large one. You may be tempted to invite everyone over in one day to get reciprocating out of the way. However, large parties cause large amounts of stress. You can play a game, chat about music, sports, and books, or do something unique with a small group.

- If it's your house, you can lead the conversation. Talk about topics you are confident in and passionate about.

o Keep the event short—mention early in the party or dinner that you'll need to end the night at a certain time because you have other things waiting for you in the morning. Adding boundaries to your activity will give you structure and make you feel more comfortable.

o Don't have dinner at your house. Instead, suggest some other ideas where you can reciprocate but not have the stress of having people in your home—prepare a picnic lunch, go out for a spa day, or do something uniquely suited for your interests. You don't have to host things at your house to reciprocate.

Give yourself some time to adapt to new practices. Don't forget to be flexible with yourself and what your friends want to do. Although you have ADHD, other people's interests and lives are just as important as yours. Building strong relationships is a way to live a healthy life, and acknowledging others is an important part of getting to your end goal with friends.

Each time you do something another person wants to do, think of it as a challenge for your ADHD. Every small step toward proving your brain isn't the end-all-be-all of power over what you desire is a victory in building the life you want.

ADHD & Romantic Relationships

Romantic relationships have difficulties, even under the best circumstances. When you throw in ADHD, you will add another spice to the mix. ADHD symptoms can lead to misunderstandings, frustration, and resentment. These feelings are not only unpleasant, but can place extra stress on each person in the couple.

A successful romantic relationship means you consistently bring attention and focus to your partner. You have to listen, support, and interact with them to show that you care. An ADHD symptomatic mind will actively work against these things if you cannot readjust to meet your partner's needs.

Disorganization, forgetfulness, and inattentiveness will have a negative effect on your relationship if it is not maintained. If your partner does not have ADHD, they may take your actions (or lack of) in the wrong way and can misinterpret intentions, resulting in resentment or frustration.

However, if you are aware of your ADHD and actively working to manage your symptoms, you can avoid more calamitous problems by adding a few steps to your treatment plan.

How Partnership is Affected

The confusion in an intimate relationship can begin when you shift from hyperfocus on your partner to inattention—since your brain is wired to tune out many consistent things in your life, having a relationship can be one of those. For example, once you lay in bed after a long day, think about how comfortable it feels to have the blankets wrap around you and the pillow cushion your head—but it's not like that every day, even when you're relaxed and feeling the comfort overtake you, eventually, the sensation fades away. This feeling is similar to having someone always around. Your brain is going to flip through that which seems perpetual and move on to other items that provide more stimulation.

It can be exciting, engaging, and interactive when a relationship is new. As each unique aspect of your partner is revealed, it's like a mystery unraveled. The early stages of a relationship can help generate feelings of love, connection, and validation. There is a deep-rooted connection that you cannot get enough of. This message becomes muddled as your focus shifts as you seek new stimuli to get that jolt of adrenaline from the instant gratification side of things.

But that doesn't last because your brain transitions quickly from one thing to the next. Once your hyperfocus on the relationship dwindles, your partner may believe you've lost interest in them or the relationship.

Even when that isn't the case.

For a woman in a serious relationship, distractions can come from the simplest of places. An example taken from CHADD.org goes something like this:

Partner without ADHD: "Hey, hon—do you want to watch a movie?"

Partner with ADHD: "Sure, I'll go make popcorn."

→ She walks to the kitchen to make popcorn but sees clothes and toys lying on the floor in the den. She picks them up and takes them to her child's room to put them away.

→ She sees that her child forgot to put their toothbrush away and left it on their desk. Even though she is annoyed with her child's inability to put things away, she picks that up and takes them to the bathroom (the clothes and toys are forgotten about).

→ When she gets to the bathroom, she realizes that it needs to be cleaned up. She pulls out the cleaning supplies and begins wiping down the counter.

→ Her partner starts looking for her throughout the house and finds her cleaning the bathroom. The partner sees her doing other things, popcorn still not made, and believes she never wanted to watch the movie in the first place.

These actions were not intentional. Her path's steady stream of distractions helped her lose her way from her original goal. If you are aware of your ADHD and have open communication with your partner about it, this instance might not be a big deal—it might even be expected. However, if your ADHD is undiagnosed, if this type of event happens often, or if you are not transparent with your partner, they may begin to see it as an issue and believe you don't want to spend time with them.

Heterosexual couples have a bigger obstacle to contend with if one partner has ADHD. If the woman in the relationship has ADHD, both partners seem to be a little happier than if it is the man with ADHD. Psychologist and Certified Sex Therapist Ari Tuckman conducted a study that showed relationships that have women with ADHD are twenty-five percent more likely to have sex with their partner than if it is the man who has ADHD. He found that women with ADHD in relationships have sex up to 73 times a year instead of the 59 times a year when a man has ADHD in the relationship. His data comes from an online survey to examine the many elements of connection and sexual gratification in couples with one ADHD partner. Tuckman's survey had seventy-two questions and received over 3000 responses.

ADHD is Different for Women

Tucker discusses his findings in the article *"It Matters Which Romantic Partner ADHD has"* on PsychologyToday.com. He found that the research shows ADHD isn't different between the sexes, but there is a definite difference in the impact between men and women with ADHD.

Tucker provides the example of height to explain. He says:

> For example, if two people are six feet tall, they have exactly the same height but would likely have a very different experience of that height depending on whether they were male or female. There are many other differences between men and women, some based on biology and some based on societal roles and expectations, which interact with ADHD to determine its impact.

> A guy who forgot a friend's birthday likely wouldn't feel as badly about it nor get as much grief as a woman who did. A lifetime of these sorts of experiences for women with ADHD may fuel self-doubt about her ability to be a good enough friend if her friends expect this kind of attention to personal details.

Because life is different for men than women, each gender will have other ADHD influences that will collide with the rest of their life. As gender roles become more flexible, there are still social expectations of what men and women "should" do.

Women are still looked at as the nurturers, caretakers, and coordinators of a household, which places a disproportionate share of the responsibilities onto their shoulders, including cleaning and childcare, especially if both partners work. Even if she has ADHD.

Suppose the male in the relationship has ADHD. In that case, it can make him less reliable about his load of the household responsibilities, which will actually fall to the woman in the relationship to pick up the slack.

The woman has to take on extra roles and responsibilities in both cases.

Another ADHD expert, Kate Kelly, author, and founder of *ADDed Dimensions Coaching*, identifies four areas of difficulty for women in intimate relationships.

- **Erratic Focus on the Relationship**: The "here today gone tomorrow" routine can be confusing and misleading. ADHD symptoms can leave a woman distracted when they wake up, only for them to become refocused for two hours, and then be off in another direction shortly thereafter. For partners, it can be uncomfortable not knowing what to expect.

- **Sensory Issues**: Women with ADHD can be sensitive to things around them, such as touching, which can feel annoying, lights that are too bright, or sounds that are too loud. When you resist being touched, it can be a big divide in the relationship.

- **Forgetfulness**: This symptom has been covered quite a bit within this book. However, Kelly states that the process of remembering is complicated for women who have ADHD. *"The first stage of memory is attending to the piece of information to be remembered. If your attention is weak, that bit of information may never make it to your brain."*

- **The Short Fuse**: People with ADHD may have a quick temper (actually, Kelly says it is pretty common). *"Their temper is activated quickly and easily. Their partner is often bewildered as the angry outburst comes from nowhere."*

Multiple studies have been conducted, and evidence has found that undiagnosed or diagnosed ADHD has less positive thoughts about intimate relationships. College students who have symptoms of ADHD report less healthy relationships than those without ADHD. Married adults with ADHD have a harder time adjusting to married life.

Sex Life

In the survey Ari Tucker conducted, he found that women with ADHD have sex more often than a man with ADHD does.

He has two hypotheses on why this is true. In his PsychologyToday.com's article, Tucker states:

I asked respondents to rate the extent to which 25 potential barriers got in the way of more frequent and/or enjoyable sex. The non-ADHD women rated more barriers as being problematic and also tended to rate the impact of those barriers as greater. For these women, this double-whammy dampened their sexual desire for their partner, more so than these potential barriers did for the guys with or without ADHD or the women with ADHD. The non-ADHD women seemed to feel these barriers more acutely and the resulting reduced desire became something of a limiting factor in the couple's sex life.

The second reason the couples with the ADHD woman have more sex is that those with ADHD tend to be more sexually eager. Therefore, although the women with ADHD may also feel that additional stress of keeping up on those obligations at home (and also in the rest of their lives), they start out with a stronger desire for sex than the women without ADHD.

So these women with ADHD start out higher and then have fewer barriers to pull down that sexual desire. At the level of group averages, this creates a convincing explanation for why these couples have sex more often than the couples where the guy has ADHD.

For a woman's perspective on women's sexuality, we also found an article from Toni Hoy, a seasoned journalist in mental health specializing in brain disorders like ADHD. She discusses how ADHD affects sex and love life.

Hoy states, *"The effects of ADHD on sexuality are highly individual and subjective, making symptoms difficult to measure. People with ADHD often struggle to keep their lives purposeful and orderly. The exhaustion that often accompanies ADHD leaves many individuals depleted of their energy."*

She describes the secondary fallout effects of ADHD between sexual interest and functioning, which can create extra stress in a marriage or romantic relationship. Some of the symptoms lead to sexual dysfunction, but when everyone involved understands ADHD and its effects on sexuality, preventative measures can be taken.

Symptoms of Sex & ADHD

Hoy separates the sexual symptoms of ADHD into two categories: Hypersexuality and Hyposexuality.

Hypersexuality indicates a high sex drive. Sexual pleasure will cause the brain to release endorphins that send neurotransmitters into action. Your brain then sends these signals to your body in response. This response causes you to feel relaxed and calm, which tends to be the opposite of how ADHD usually makes you feel.

When you engage in masturbation or intercourse, you relieve some of your stress. As this tension release mixes with the impulsivity type of ADHD, you may give in to your sexual whims frequently, adding additional problems to your intimate relationship. Sexual impulsivity can lead to unprotected sex, addiction to pornography, promiscuity, and a desire for multiple sex partners.

When impulsive ADHD goes undiagnosed, it can also open up the gateway to substance abuse and poor decision-making skills including sexual behaviors that are risky to your physical, mental, and emotional health.

Hyposexuality

This type of sexuality is the opposite of the previous kind. Instead of having an insatiable sex drive, you'll have difficulty reaching arousal during intimate physical moments. You may lose interest in sex while you are in the act, or you can just not have an interest.

Certain ADHD medications list hyposexuality as a side effect, which is more common among people who combine ADHD medication with antidepressants.

Other symptoms can include irritability after climax. This irritability can intertwine with depression or sadness since the brain is releasing less dopamine during that time.

Lack of focus may also be a problem. You may have trouble concentrating on the sensations while they go on or wish you were doing something else.

The APA does not recognize sexual symptoms as part of ADHD, including problems with promiscuity or addiction to pornography. Although they are not part of a formal diagnosis, sexual symptoms can have already impacted your health and safety.

How to Switch Gears

If you are in a relationship, when sexual symptoms occur, they can impact your partner.

Your lack of interest, constant distraction, or inability to concentrate may be viewed as signs of rejection.

To help your partners understand you better, it's important to communicate about your ADHD symptoms and explain what happens. Your inability to focus before, during, or after sex has nothing to do with your desire for your partner or your interest in them—it's a matter of not being able to concentrate.

If you have been living with an undiagnosed case of ADHD, your family and partner may have a difficult time understanding what is happening with your forgetfulness, frustration, and anger. The symptoms of ADHD can directly and dramatically affect your relationships with people, including in the sexual arena.

While your sexuality depends on the hyper- or hypo- type, you may still find discomfort with hypersensitivity in the bedroom. Sights, sounds, smells, and your environment can create sensory overload where you cannot focus on enjoying your sexual experience.

Although women with hyposexuality may have a difficult time climaxing, or feeling much pleasure at all, if you experience hyperactive ADHD, you will feel as though you are in non-stop overdrive. If this type of ADHD is your significant symptom, you may find that you are always looking for a quick encounter sexually. Your partner may want to do things differently.

Getting on the same page and switching gears to realize that you and your partner need to enjoy the event will better understand what you both want and can open your intimacy up to a new level.

To build up communication, you can try some of these items:

- **Talk things out.** Let your partner know how your ADHD affects you and could impact certain intimate experiences. Listen to your partner about their insecurities and desires as well. Talk before, during, and after sex to describe what and how you feel and what level of intimacy you are looking to achieve.

- **Mix things up.** Try some things you haven't tried before—with permission from your partner. Look at new positions or locations and buy books on how to improve intimacy. Consensual sex and adventures are the only way to fly in this scenario. If your partner is less adventurous than you are, you must respect their wishes. If you do not want to try something, but your partner does, make sure to set that boundary as the one you are uncomfortable with. Sex is only fun if both people are comfortably enjoying it.

- <u>Focus on mutually satisfying one another</u>. Don't avoid sex because you are afraid of being intimate or scared that one of your symptoms will ruin the mood. If you need to schedule sex into your routine, then you should do so and be willing to keep the appointment when it comes around. When it is time to engage in physical activity, use mindfulness to get you in the mood. Do some calming exercises during foreplay. You can turn on the sound of the ocean, meditate, or do yoga. Work to focus on your partner and be present.

- <u>Seek out a professional</u>. Experts in the area or therapists who have experience with ADHD and other brain disorders can help your partner develop a plan. Not all therapists are created equally. You are not going to mesh with every therapist you meet. Instead, you might have to try a few people out before finding the best counselor that will suit your personality. However, you have to really give therapy a good try before moving on to someone else. You will have good and bad days with therapy, and the goal is to help you grow and become the person you've always wanted to be.

Friendly Advice

Now that we've laid out all the issues that come into play with ADHD and social life, we want to give you some ways to guide your way through the rough patches because you can! ADHD is manageable and can become your greatest asset if you figure out how to work it with your lifestyle. See the advice below.

- Ari Tucker says to make your life different and better, release the gender role expectations from your relationships. Especially in your romantic partnerships. Divide up the housework and childcare responsibilities evenly between the two of you. This way, you (or your partner) don't have to feel resentful about having to shoulder the burden alone.

- To create healthy relationships, you can:

  ○ Identify harmful behaviors that can derail your relationships.

  ○ Build routine check-ups into your structure for a friend or romantic partner.

  ○ Address issues as they happen.

  ○ Reinforce your partner's strengths (and they should reinforce yours).

  ○ Remember your romantic relationship is important.

    ▪ Schedule a date night.

    ▪ Schedule time to talk about relationship connections.

    ▪ Schedule time to discuss rebuilding your relationship.

    ▪ Schedule a time for fun and laughter. Celebrate each other.

  ○ Learn to be patient with one another.

    ▪ Give positive feedback each day.

    ▪ Lift each other up.

    ▪ Understand that change on both ends is going to take time. Your partner may not automatically understand your ADHD symptoms, just as you may not get everything buttoned up and straightened around on the first try.

  ○ Facts and feelings are different. Learn how to separate them during high-level emotional moments.

    ▪ If your feelings are hurt and you're going to blow up, communicate your need to remove yourself from the conversation and come back to it once you've calmed down. Nothing is ever resolved by screaming and yelling at one another.

  ○ Be a better communicator.

- Don't be afraid to see professional help.

- Focus on the discussion.

- Spend time together uninterrupted and without distractions.

- Speak face-to-face when talking about serious issues and look people in the eye when you do so.

o   Catch yourself in the ADHD trigger moments.

- If you feel like your mind just shut down or sped up, remove yourself from the situation. If you have prominent symptoms once you are working on your treatment plan, pay attention to the times when your symptoms are heightened. This knowledge can help you with communication in the long-term.

Conclusion

Being in any relationship is a difficult thing to do. ADHD does add another dynamic to the friendship, but if you are honest with yourself and your friends, you'll be able to maneuver around those symptoms and have them work for you in no time.

In the next chapter, we discuss ADHD, career challenges and tips.

CHAPTER EIGHT

ADHD & Your Career

"Think like a queen. A queen is not afraid to fail. Failure is just another stepping stone to greatness."
~ ~ Oprah

Finding something that will keep your interest can be difficult when you have ADHD (and may not know it yet). And, when a project, task, or job doesn't hold your interest, chances are you're either quitting it or becoming so scattered the job may have some serious repercussions.

Although working in an office seems like a good opportunity, being there may often feel difficult. You may need to take a lot of breaks, have a miss-mash of disorganization between your desk, drawers, and computer, or you may just have a hard time concentrating when other people are around. This problem can lead to you spending long hours at work just to get some quiet time and have an ability to focus.

The impact ADHD has on your career can be huge. If you find that you cannot work in an office because sitting in one place drives you bonkers or that you can't meet a project deadline, your self-esteem may plummet. This downslide can severely undervalue yourself, which means that you'll take a job below your skill and pay level because you don't think you can do anything more.

But, that's not the case.

If you are experiencing any type of mental health difficulty, your days may be filled with confusion, discomfort, and miscommunication. If you are dead set on sticking with the office job, it's time to talk to your manager about getting support throughout the workplace.

You are probably not the only person struggling with some form of neurodiversity in your chosen field, and positive adjustments can be used to support all individuals.

However, the foremost rule of working is to look for something you are passionate about.

You do not have to jump headfirst into a new career because you read this book. But, having a job where you are treated well, comfortable, and challenged will be a great way to keep your ADHD at bay.

If you are in a job or career where you are dissatisfied, it's time to start looking for something that keeps your interest better.

To find a job that suits you better, you can take small steps; update your resume, post it on social media job platforms, or only career platforms. And then take a few interviews. When you do, you ask the questions. You develop the type of career you want to have and find a company or position that suits your needs.

Yes. We all need money.

Yes. You can't always just fall into the perfect career—especially if you have ADHD.

BUT, you can take on a "pay the bills" gig while you figure out what you really want to do.

The most important question to ask yourself is: What do you really want to be doing?

If you do not know, that is okay, and there are many ways to find out what is the right fit for you. If you know but don't think your career choice is viable or possible, tell that voice to stuff it. Anything is possible.

You just have to find the right pieces to your puzzle.

Your "Pay The Bills" Job

If you are already working a "pay the bills" job and find it hard to stay focused on any given day, create a sense of camaraderie in your workplace for mental health days and build mental health support groups.

If you've gotten your formal ADHD diagnosis and are working on your behavioral treatment plan, talk to your manager or management staff and develop some new strategies to go along with your work life.

The fact of the matter is that you are a good employee, and to get the best effort out of you, you'll have to put some procedures in place so you can produce the highest-quality work possible.

If you are in the "pay the bills" job stage and management refuses to work with you to better your ADHD management, know that there are other "pay the bills" jobs in the world. You don't have to work in a crappy place because you need to make money.

Some places support you as you are and try to bolster the most out of you through compassion, understanding, and guidance toward a better life for you.

If it turns out that you are highly driven by money, and the current job you have is a well-paying one that may not treat employees as well as they could, but you're okay with the money as motivation—that's okay too.

The key is finding what works right for you in the short- and long-term.

Short-Term "Pay the Bills" Job

- Anything that helps you get by in your daily life. This job can be less challenging but helps free your mind so you can begin carving out a career path long-term.

- Can be flexible or set hours.

- It tends to be a job you don't "take home" with you.

- Low on stress (even if some situations present themselves as stressful at certain times).

- Supportive co-workers, staff, and management teams.

- Helps provide you with food, clothes, a roof over your head, and medical benefits.

- Someplace you form friendships but not necessarily feel connected or chained to for your life.

Long-Term Career Goals

- Answer the hard question of, "What do I want to do?"

- Do a little research once you find an answer—it does not have to be a permanent solution. If you think you might be interested in something, check it out. Talk to some people in the profession, and see what a career path looks like.

- Get in on the ground floor. If you like music and want to work in the music industry, you may have to start as a receptionist or an assistant to get your luck in. Jumping in at entry-level means you learn every aspect of the profession. If you aren't interested in putting your energy into something because it is too simple, the profession might not be for you.

- Look into classes and schools that offer degrees on the subject you're interested in. See what the degree is about by talking with a recruitment agent, a department professor, and students who major in the subject you are interested in. If it is a public school, you can also audit a class for free, just to see if it is up to your alley.

ADHD doesn't limit you. It probably gives you a better opportunity to tackle more things at one time than it seems. However, you do have to start someplace. Taking small steps toward a longer goal is a great way to work your ADHD management into your career life.

Long-Term Passion Careers

One reason you might not pursue a long-term passion as a career is low self-esteem due to ADHD. A high number of the population doesn't follow their career dreams because of low-self esteem. You don't have to be one of those people. However, you may have some taller hurdles to jump over. Extra challenges don't mean that you shouldn't try or do what you want. You have to find the right way to make things work for you.

Some of the challenges you may have to overcome can include:

- Constructive criticism (learning how to accept it)

- Difficulty with intrapersonal relationships

- Disorganization

- Forgetfulness

- Inattention

- Taking compliments with grace

These are all the items you may already know you have issues with. But, these conflicts may be exacerbated at work, especially if you have comorbid disorders.

A new level comes into play when you have to invite other people (co-workers) into the world of your mental health struggles. As it is a professional life, you don't have to put yourself where your colleagues will know every bit of information about you. However, clear communication can help them understand why you react certain ways to specific stimuli.

In an article titled *"ADHD in the Workplace—The Impact on Woman,"* a Chief Medical Officer of Onebright, Gabrielle Pendlebury, suggests other beneficial systems that can help women with ADHD. Some of the most targeted support can help women manage their feelings of distress and stress, manage or regulate your emotions, help you cope with feelings of isolation or rejection, and can help manage interpersonal conflict.

It can also provide training for building assertiveness, learning how to compromise, improving the outcome of your occupation, coping with everyday social interactions, and giving you some negotiation guidelines.

Pendlebury advises enrolling a Mental Health Champion. If not you, speak with your manager and discuss mental health as a serious issue that can be improved upon.

Mental Health Champions can be one person or a group of people who can help support and guide others to the best option for their mental health. If your organization doesn't have a support network, suggest building one. If they have a mental health network, think about joining it as a member or a champion (or both). Having a peer-to-peer system in place can help you, and all other colleagues develop a more understanding and adaptable environment where you can manage your ADHD in the open instead of hiding it in the shadows.

If you are not comfortable with forming or joining a mental health task force (at least initially), there are some other adjustments that you can make with your management team with little to no fanfare.

In 2010, the Equality Act was put into place. This act states that you are protected should you choose to disclose your learning disorder. If you choose to do so in a confidential (or non-confidential) way, your employer has a legal duty to make reasonable adjustments for you and others who reveal neurodivergence.

If you are at a workplace, know that you have the legal right to maneuver your job function to suit your individual needs. The change in process may include adding an extra step to the process, extra equipment, or a switch in the pattern of how you work. You may have to try a few things before the right work habits form, but with the proper steps involved, you can do your job really well.

Positives of Work and ADHD

Your thoughts ping-pong all over your brain, sometimes they can be described as "racing" other times, and it might be hard to hear anything at all. Regardless of how your brain absorbs information, your mind is going to come up with unique solutions to problems and out-of-the-box-ideas for innovation. You have some really great things to show your colleagues and employers.

Those who have ADHD have been noted for seeing things further, having an intense sense of observation, and creative energy that others are unable to offer.

Your business or organization should be as accommodating as they can be toward you.

Giving you an opportunity to thrive in your environment will open up possibilities that the company may not have had otherwise. You thrive when multitasking and can give intense attention on projects when your interest is focused.

Find Your Chosen Career

Not everyone does what they love. But, you can, and you should.

A career is something that you're passionate about. When you do something you have interest in, you're going to invest in it with everything you have. This statement is especially true if you have ADHD.

The biggest challenge with your ADHD may not be managing the symptoms you have, it might be finding interesting work to do. For example, if you get a job as an executive assistant, but have no desire to manage someone's personal or professional life, you're going to struggle with easy tasks like picking up dry cleaning, or scheduling appointments.

It's the struggle you're going to want to avoid.

When we struggle, we make mistakes, when we make mistakes, we start to get down on ourselves, which affects our self-esteem, and snowballs into some other emotional problems that can be exacerbated by the ADHD brain.

Billy Roberts LISW-S and therapist at Focused Mind ADHD Counseling have found that, *"If pointed in the right direction, ADHD can be a superpower."*

The Journal of Attention Disorders published a study that discovered those with ADHD had more real-world creative achievements than those without. This study also revealed ADHD adults choose more creative tasks and environments to build their skillset to mirror their preferences.

If you don't know what you want to do, you're not alone. There are people, books, and assessments you can take to get your career juices flowing—even some online that are free to begin to get an idea of what you're interested in and best suited for.

Before you jump into any of the assessments, you'll need to look inward and self-reflect. If you get a notebook, you can answer the following questions. (Writing the questions and answers down will help you visualize them better, they'll also allow you to see them, so you don't forget them.)

- What can you spend hours talking about or researching?

- What would you prefer to do with your weekend time?

- Can you work in a team, or do you choose to work individually?

- Do you like to be in charge? Are you comfortable taking the lead?

- What bothers you the most about people, places, and things (what are your pet peeves)?

- Do you prefer fast- or slow-paced environments?

- What activities drain you, and which ones excite you?

- What job would you love to do if money wasn't an issue?

To find the best job for your unique ADHD brain, you need to figure out what lights your fire.

~~ BILLY ROBERTS, LISW-S

I don't want to leave you with no ideas of what could be your possible career, and in the next section, I've found some great possible occupations for women who have ADHD. However, answering the questions above, and being honest with yourself, will get you one step closer to the best way to love what career you're in.

Best Jobs for ADHD Minds

You have many unique qualities, and because of the way you problem-solve, create systems, and have the superpower of multitasking, your ADHD mind will lend itself well to work in creative fields, computer programming, or entrepreneurship. Other roles women with ADHD can find success in (and would love to do) are:

- Artist

- Athlete

- Beautician

- Chef

- Computer technician

- Copy editor

- Daycare worker

- Emergency Medical Technician (EMT), first responder

- Engineer

- Hair Stylist

- High-tech field

- Hospitality management or industry

- Journalist

- Nurse

- Sales representative (not in a call center)

- Small business owner

- Software engineer

- Stage management in the theater

- Teacher

Of course, these are only some ideas, and you can do whatever drives you and makes you feel whole. Those with ADHD tend to do well with non-traditional or flexible schedules. Other things to consider are how well you thrive under pressure and stay calm in fast-paced environments like hospitals, restaurants, and classrooms.

Stay Motivated With ADHD

Finding a job you love is only half the battle. No matter what position you are in, you're probably going to experience cognitive issues.

A study conducted by Anselm B.M. Fuernaier, a director at the department of clinical and developmental neuropsychology at the University of Groningen in the Netherlands, and their team conducted a study on *"ADHD at the Workplace: ADHD Symptoms, diagnostic status, and work-related functioning."* They found that up to 69% of those with ADHD reported impairments in finishing work efficiently and working to their full potential. This study also discovered that up to 23% of people with ADHD reported issues with getting fired or had problems with attending their job.

Cognitive issues you may experience could be:

- Forgetting important details, even though you actively listened to the conversation.

- Becoming overwhelmed by checking your emails.

- A feeling of hopelessness when attempting to finish essential tasks.

- A consistent tardiness issue, even if you wake up early.

- Feelings of unproductiveness, even when you work longer hours than your co-workers.

While none of these issues make you a bad employee, you may overlook the fact that they are challenges you have to work with. Instead, try to maintain your motivation by staying productive and avoiding boredom.

Some things you can do at any job are:

- **Build a routine.** Not every task you do at your job (even if it is a dream job) will motivate you. That doesn't mean it shouldn't be done, even if you have ADHD.

When you build a routine that includes daily and fundamental tasks, you can stay on track, get the boring work out of the way, and move on to the things that inspire you most.

With ADHD, it is easy to become hyper-focused on tasks that aren't beneficial for what needs to be done in the present moment, which is why building vital tasks into your routine can help you avoid not accomplishing the more mundane tasks.

- **List out your expectations**. What do you expect from yourself at work? How do you want to be viewed? Do you want to be the leader people turn to, or would you prefer to work hard behind the scenes?

Would you like to get to work on time for five days in a row? Would you want to make sure to complete a specific project one day before the actual deadline?

Writing down your expectations allows you to see what you want for yourself and keep it in mind. It gives you a roadmap to feeling good about your work.

When you keep the expectations in your sightline, at least daily, you'll get a chance to have the ideas fresh for you, which will guide you to keep going and give you a great goal to reach.

- **Energize to the max**. You have probably had bursts of energy where you can step back and be proud of what you accomplished only to take one more step back and realize how laser-focused you became that you forgot to do other, crucial projects. Leaning on larger creative projects is a great thing to do when you're trying to maximize your energy. Think about volunteering for this kind of work project to encourage the most production possible.

Take advantage of these projects and moments. If you're getting these bursts of energy during certain times out of the day, work these surges into your schedule. When you do this, you are essentially creating time to hyper-focus on something that needs to get done.

- **Set goals**. Every place you work is going to have goals set for your production. If you work in fast food, your goals may consist of making so many hamburgers in one hour. If you work in retail, maybe you'll have to get a certain number of credit card applicants each day. If you're an artist, you'll have deadlines to meet.

Although your supervisor will set certain goals for you to meet, when you have ADHD, it should work best when you break those goals into smaller tasks and create self-imposed targets to meet.

If you are comfortable talking to your employer about your ADHD, ask them for adjustments or changes on goals that cause anxiety. Work together to ensure productivity and completion of tasks.

If your ADHD works best when you have a competitor, try to enlist the help of a co-worker to compete against. Should you be unable to find someone, you can always compete against yourself by looking to have the best time with minimal mistakes.

Entrepreneurs and those who work for themselves can use SMART goals to help them build a plan or compete against themselves. These goals will provide you with flexibility and help create achievable goals.

<u>SMART goals are</u>:

- o Specific

- o Measurable

- o Attainable

- o Relevant

- o Timely

Creating these SMART goals can help you keep your work in line.

- o **Specific goals** are defined as narrow goals that can be effective in planning.

- o **Measurable goals** are defined as something you can calculate to see that you're making progress on your project. (For example, if you're a writer, you'll have a daily goal of writing 5000 words, five days a week.)

- o **Attainable goals** are defined as reasonable goals that can be reached in a certain timeline.

- **Relevant goals** are defined as an alignment of project values and long-term objectives to complete the task at hand.

- **Timely goals** are defined as the realistic, time-oriented purpose that will motivate, drive, and prioritize the tasks at hand.

When you are trying to write down your SMART goals, you may not clearly understand how to do it until you get used to creating them. See the ideas below to help you develop the right type of SMART goal for your project or task at hand.

- When developing your **specific goals**, you'll need definite answers to questions like:

  - What do you need to accomplish?

  - Who bears the responsibility?

  - How can we achieve this goal?

These questions will help you get to the bottom of your end goal.

- When developing **measurable goals**, you'll be looking for something to "count." For example, if your goal is to grow how many people use your employer's app, you'll have to ask these questions:

  - How many people do you want the user number to grow by?

  - What timeline do you expect the numbers to increase by?

  - What is the outcome if you do not reach that number?

  - If you have even one person sign up, that is a positive step in reaching your goal.

  - What type of methods can you use to reach your goal (ex: advertising, updates, etc.)

o   What are the benchmarks that will track the goal? (Meaning, what are the small plans to reach the end goal?

- When you establish the **achievable goals**, you'll be looking to give yourself a dose of reality. The achievable goals should all be realistic, not something that is out of reach. To ensure that your goals are achievable, ask yourself the following questions:

  o   Is the object of the goal something you can accomplish?

  o   Is the timeline you wish to accomplish the goal reasonable?

  o   Can you reach the end goal in the timeline you've provided?

- To create **relevant goals**, you'll want to think about the whole picture. Ask yourself: Why set the goals you're selecting when you set them?

- The **timely goals** may seem easy to understand, but make sure you ask yourself these questions when setting them:

  o   What is your timeline?

  o   What are the smaller benchmarks to review progress on a project?

  o   Is your timeline feasible? Are you pushing time just to get a project done? If the deadline isn't attainable, readjust if you can.

SMART goals provide deadlines and parameters to help you tackle your assignments routinely and timely. This type of goal setting also allows you to work well with any cognitive problems your ADHD may bring up.

- **Take breaks**. Everyone needs to cut themselves some slack and step away from a task. The human body and mind can only be pushed so far. When you take a break, you allow your mind and body to replenish their energy stores. ADHD will affect the chemistry of your brain and the ability to sustain attention. Track how often you can maintain focus on daily, weekly, and one-time tasks. Take a break when you feel or see your attention start to wane. It can be for five minutes or fifteen—each person needs different breaks for additional time.

When you find that your attention fades around forty-five minutes, begin to set the alarm to remind you that it's time to swerve your attention to calling a friend, eating lunch, going for a walk, etc. Keep your breaks around the same time when you are working, so you can begin to train your mind on how to respond to a lack of attention.

If you go at full speed for too long, you'll begin to burn out, leading to longer periods of unproductivity. These periods can be places where your self-esteem plummets.

Instead of pushing yourself 24/7, make breaks and mental health days a priority.

Conclusion

If you don't love your job and you have ADHD, you may grow unfocused and bored. The lack of motivation may have you believe that you're a "bad" employee, which can't be further from the truth. Instead, you're not engaged enough with the job you are at. Someone with ADHD needs to be challenged and interested in most aspects of the work they are paid for. Because of this, if you have ADHD or suspect you have it, you should begin asking yourself some tough questions about what you are passionate about. (These questions are only tough if you don't know what to do and aren't used to listening to your instincts.)

The fact of the matter is that when engaged or interested in your work, you run the risk of becoming a workaholic, which is why you should implement routines, goals, and healthy habits into your work life and your personal life.

The next chapter will discuss ADHD and how to have a healthy relationship with money.

CHAPTER NINE

ADHD & Financial Health

Introduction

If you have ADHD, you may have issues with money. Impulsivity and that search for that shot of dopamine with instant gratification can spur an unhealthy balance of shopping sprees and owning material possessions. This behavior can also lead to hoarding, clutter, and poor money management.

If you forget things when they are out of sight, you may also have a hard time paying bills on time or at all. These instances can lead you down a road of debt where it is almost impossible to dig yourself out of.

All aspects of spending too much and not paying bills can have serious repercussions on your personal life and relationships with people. If you are a mother and have children, even those who don't have ADHD, you may pass down your poor money skills to them—children model what their parents do.

There are many reasons to get your financial health in order, and one of the biggest ones is the stress and frantic energy that comes with the thought of yet another bill coming in the mail or going unpaid.

When you sort through your money problems and get them tidied up, you're relieving yourself from the strain of future issues, modeling good behavior for children, and organizing your home, so your ADHD doesn't exacerbate itself.

You are in control of this, and you just have to come up with a plan. This chapter will help you discover what kind of relationship you have with money, what to do about debt, how to save and spend for the future, and how to build a money schedule.

Let's get started.

Your Relationship With Your Money

Managing money is an important skill to develop. It might be harder with ADHD, but it's not impossible.

Once you master your spending habits and create a financial schedule, the days of always having a low checking account, no savings account, and creditors calling you can wash away. Instead, you'll be able to get the loan you were looking for, and your utilities will always be on.

When thinking about finances, the first thing you have to look at is your relationship with money. Every person with ADHD may have a different connection to how they deal with their money, but it doesn't mean that it wasn't a problem for them at one point.

Some of your issues may include:

- You avoid paying bills.

- You do not organize bills, tax papers, checks, etc.

- You procrastinate on paying bills, which incur more late fees than they are worth.

- You cannot manage to save money for emergencies, vacations, or the future.

- You don't keep track of your expenses or your bank balance.

- You continually make large purchases on credit cards, which increasingly go up due to late payments and interest rates.

If any of these things sound familiar, you probably have a little (or a lot) of stress when you think about finances.

Do You Know Where Your Money Goes?

The idea is simple, and if you flip through your memories of the stuff you purchased last week, you might have a clue where some of your money has gone. But, having a record of what you spend can help you with any impulsive spending you're tempted to do.

If you have a pen and small notebook with you at all times (or use an app on your phone), you can record any purchases you have. Then, once a day or week, you can register your spending on a sheet that gives you insight into what you spend weekly or monthly. You might be surprised at how much your spending will cut down when you have a visual number to reference.

Keeping track of your spending includes groceries, sundries, online purchases, gas, eating out, clothes, and more. Any time you use your card, you need to track it.

When you first begin this practice, it might be hard for you to focus because it can be annoying to sit in one place and put numbers into small boxes, but remind yourself that you are doing it for a reason. The reason becomes clear the longer you do it, and the more you see yourself spending or saving.

Don't worry if you miss a few installments here and there, the goal is for you to build a habit of tracking your expenses on the whole. This way, you'll develop a better relationship with your money.

Anyone who lives in your household should keep track of their money. If it is just you alone, then hold yourself accountable by asking a family member or friend to check in with this project just to make sure you continue keeping track. If you live with a partner or spouse, have them track their money. At the end of the week or the month, you should sit down and see where their money went and where your money has gone.

When you track your spending, include fixed and variable expenses. Fixed expenses include housing, loans, transportation, and utilities—they tend to be the same amount every month. Variable costs include clothing, entertainment, food, gas, and other items that can vary, price-wise, from month to month. For example, the month before school, you may spend more money on clothes for your children because they have grown out of their other clothes. Next month, you probably won't be spending as much.

Include expenses that come around every few months, like homeowner association fees, yearly subscriptions, taxes, and memberships.

What Are Your Goals?

When you start situating your financial health, you'll need to look at your goals.

Reflect on what you'd like your financial future to look like. These goals will include short- and long-term intentions. If you have a partner or spouse, incorporate their ideas into the discussion.

First, write down your short-, mid-, and long-term thoughts about what you'd like to do with your money. Short-term goals can include eating out less, keeping financial papers organized, or saving a specific amount each week. Mid-term goals can consist of going on a special vacation, buying a piece of new furniture, or paying off one credit card. Long-term goals can include saving up for college or adding money to a retirement fund.

Once you get an idea, you can create a vision board with future items you'd like to purchase, which can give you the motivation to save up for them. Otherwise, you can sort your list into essential and non-essential supplies and then ask yourself a few questions:

1) What are the top three to five must-haves on your essential list?

2) What are your top three to five must-haves on your non-essential list?

3) What is your current financial status?

4) What is stopping you from having a healthy economic life?

5) Where would you like to see yourself financially in one, three, and five years?

When you've answered these questions, you'll find your problem spots. Then, you can resolve some of the money-related issues you've had with spending and saving.

To help this process work with your ADHD brain, break your goals into smaller steps that you can tackle daily, weekly, monthly, or yearly. If you have a hard time organizing goals or keeping to a specific target amount, ask a family member, friend, coach, or therapist for help. Don't be afraid to ask people who might know more about this subject and can get you on the right path.

Successfully managing money means that you'll have to pay attention to all goals. Each one you set is a crucial part of your financial health.

Your Debt

Debt piles up quickly.

Everyone has issues at one time or another with debt. There are good debts like smart investments and home loans—things that will improve your fiscal health— and there are bad debts like credit card bills—debts that cannot be recovered, as in they are lost forever once you pay them.

For a woman with ADHD, impulse spending can be a problem. Impulse spending can be large purchases, like a laptop, or small, like a pack of gum at a check-out line. Although impulse spending can be a challenge, when you curb that desire to buy, for whatever reason, you're choosing a better way to be fiscally responsible.

To start, you can tame your impulses by doing a few of these things:

- **Click 'unsubscribe.'** These darn emails send a bunch of sales and specials to your inbox. It's hard to know exactly where they come from all the time, but companies market emails to be directed to what you will purchase. Retail emails are designed to get your attention and to have you buy—if you unsubscribe from them, you'll be able to resist online purchases much easier.

- **Keep track of what you spend while you shop.** Keeping track of your weekly and monthly expenses helps you know where your money is, and keeping track of what you are paying at the moment can help hold yourself accountable while you're shopping, especially if you go to more than one store.

- **Learn what your temptations are, and come up with a plan to stay away**

from them. This step calls for you to be honest with yourself. Look at your spending habits, and find where you are most likely to purchase something impulsively. Do you go to the mall often? Do you like to frequent the arts and crafts store with nothing particular in mind? Online retailers can also lead to impulse buys. When you know what triggers your spending, you can create a plan to get the inclination for even small purchases down to a minimum.

- **Look for things to do locally that are free or inexpensive.** Look for peer groups, libraries, museums, clubs, parks, etc., to keep yourself entertained on a budget. Many public parks have leagues you can join or exercise groups to participate in. Keeping yourself entertained with free or low-cost activities can curb your spending substantially.

- **Make things a little harder on yourself.** Keep the credit cards at home. Bring the lowest amount of money you think you will need, and you'll help keep your money where it belongs.

- **Sit back and wait.** Want to buy a big purchase and are worried it will sell out or that the sale will go away too soon? It doesn't matter why you want to purchase a bigger item, and I suggest that you sit back and wait.

Find an amount of time that feels right, like twenty-four hours, and wait to purchase your item. If, after the time passes, you have the money, and you still want the bigger object, then you can buy it. However, you may realize (even if you have the money) that the purchase isn't needed right now.

- **Use a shopping list and stick to the items on it.** There will be times when you make a list and forget one ingredient for dinner. If you do, it's okay to buy that ingredient, but steer clear of going down the isles where you don't need something or purchasing a new food just because you're curious to try it. One of the biggest offenders that motivate impulse buying is junk food—especially if you're in a bad mood or have a moment where you feel vulnerable.

Vulnerability leads to that needed dose of dopamine, and when you're shopping, that can be a super trigger. If you find yourself shopping in an emotional mood, it's best to come back to the task later when you're feeling more grounded and focused.

Do you need help? Have someone hold you accountable for your spending habits, and enlist the help of a friend or family member to keep you in check when you don't feel as though you can do it alone.

Your Credit Cards

Credit cards are great for emergencies and when you need something small, but spending can easily spiral out of control if you miss a payment or don't pay off the total right away. Interest, late, and over-the-limit fees can really screw everything up. If you are someone who pays only a minimum amount on a large credit card bill, it can take you thirty years to pay off the balance in full.

If you have issues paying credit card bills, it's time to ask yourself if you really should be using them. Sit back and pause when you buy something using a credit card. If you can't pay the card right off, you don't have the money to buy what you're thinking about. If that isn't enough motivation, ask yourself if you want to spend the next thirty years paying it off—is the item worth that much to you?

Credit cards are purposefully easy. This ease promotes impulse buys, makes it difficult for people to save money, and encourages you to use a card even when you could easily use cash. The credit card companies want to be able to charge you interest, so they are making money.

If you still think you need help, talk to a friend or family member. Have them be part of your support team.

Planning for the Future

You're going to need money in the future too.

Having and adding to a savings account is an amazing thing you can do for your family, yourself, and your future. Savings are honestly a great way to plan to pay for an emergency. You can put as much or as little into your savings to prepare for your future, but you actually have the money to do it.

If you haven't started a savings account yet, open one with your local bank and start small. Put a little of your paycheck in a savings account each time you get paid. Technology makes direct depositing into separate accounts (one for checking, another into savings) so you won't even have to think about it. One great idea is to not request a debit card for the savings account. If you don't have an easy way to access the money, you'll have to stop and think about spending it.

Do you have something in mind that you'd like to save for? If so, create a vision board with decorations to amp yourself up for saving money. You can even make a chart or graph that makes saving fun for you (for example, the more the pie is filled in, the closer you are to reaching your goal).

If you're looking to save on a short-term basis, you can get a jar or envelope and put the money into it. Glue an image of what you are saving for on the outside, so you're constantly reminded why the money is there and what is important enough to save that amount.

Create Your Spending Plan

Building a spending plan will help you map out the expenses you have that are upcoming for the week, month, and year. You can include everything, including a lump sum for incidentals, utilities, and loan payments. You can funnel these items into a monthly plan since they are paid once a month. This method is often referred to as "spending the money before you get it." That idea means you already know where your paycheck is going and how much you need it to go to each place.

You'll be less likely to spend the money impulsively when you know where each amount goes.

Some of the elements you'll need to incorporate into a monthly budget are:

- **Figure out how much money you need each month.** Calculate all bills and expenses into this number. Once you have it, write it down so you can see it. If you like spreadsheets for organization, this task would be great to add your money to.

- **Find what works best for you**. Remember, all ADHD symptoms look a little different in each person. You may have to try a few ways before you get the right budget for your life.

- **Make a master list**. Use the total amount of purchases from the last twelve months to see what you've spent. If you've kept track in your checkbook, you can use that for the numbers. Otherwise, your bank should have statements online or ready to print out for you at a brick-and-mortar location.

- **Look back twelve months**. Add up all spending done in the last year. Divide that number by twelve to see what your average monthly expenses are. Use that idea as a reference point for the next few months and tweak it if needed.

- **Use online platforms to help**. Many platforms can help you keep your budget in check. Money management programs like Mint and Quicken can help you gather this information and keep it in one place. Excel also has some cool tools to help you do math without actually doing the math each time you add something new.

- **Review all your spending each week**. Settle on one day of the week to analyze your spending. Find out if you are on a budget for the month and check to see what bills are upcoming for the next week. Look through your monthly plan to see what is happening next. When looking through forthcoming expenses, you can write notes to remind you what comes next, when to mail bills out, and how much budget you have left for the month.

- **Make technology work for you**. There are many ways to pay bills, and now you can pay them electronically too. If you are confident in your budget-keeping skills, you can create electronic payments that come out automatically at the same time each month. However, if you don't have that money in your account, it can cause a host of other problems. If you don't trust yourself with automatic payments, email reminders are great visual tools and can still be paid electronically (which saves time, energy, and the environment).

- **Build your savings**. Make deposits into a separate account, so you have a little money saved up. This money can help with emergencies and be used for special events or bigger items.

- **Create a financial calendar**. You have ADHD. Your ADHD needs something visual to remember them. Having a calendar in your line of vision each day can give you that boost of visualization along with financial responsibility.

If these things don't work for you, you can always look into money management apps and research other helpful tricks online, with a coach, at a bank, and more.

Managing Money Through a Schedule

To manage ADHD, your best bet is to create routines. Making a schedule for money management will fall in line with these daily, weekly, and monthly habits you create for yourself.

Timelines are helpful ways to get your money organized through financial tasks and how frequently things need to be completed. Each task should have a timeframe of how long you believe it will take to finish—finding out that certain jobs like paying bills can motivate you to do them more often. Fit your timeline into your lifestyle and line them up with your goals. This type of money management system can help you discover what needs to be done and when it needs to be done.

<u>**An example timeline could look like this**</u>:

Every day—

- Gather receipts spent during the day. Find them on your desk or in your pockets, wallet, car, etc. This task should take five minutes.

- Enter the receipts into your spreadsheet and place them into an envelope to be reviewed at the end of each month. This task should take five minutes.

- Open any bills that came that day, and write the date each bill needs to be mailed in order to arrive by the due date. Place them in a basket and organize them by the date they need to be paid. Keep this basket in a place where you can see it frequently. This task should take five minutes.

One day a week—

- Pay bills. Write "PAID" on the stub and add the date you wrote the check. Put that paperwork in a folder labeled "Paid Bills." Put the pills in order by the date they were paid. Shred last month's bills as you pay this month's bills. This task should take ten minutes.

- Look through your inbox for automatic notification payments that are upcoming or have been paid in the last week. Add them to your money management system (i.e., checkbook finance software). This task should take ten minutes.

- Review your weekly expenses. Look at what you expect to spend within the next week. This task should take five minutes.

- Visit your bank to withdraw any cash needed for the week and deposit any checks you have. If the bank you use has a mobile app, you might be able to skip going to the bank and deposit checks by photo. This task depends on the travel time to your bank and how busy the bank is.

Once a month—

- Balance your checking account. Use online tools or checkbooks to make sure what you have in the bank is what you have on your end too. Compare what is spent to what is deposited with your records. Balance your account to ensure that you or your bank didn't make any mistakes. This task should take twenty minutes.

- Shred any receipts after your bank account is balanced. This task should take ten minutes.

- Compare your budget and goals to what has actually been spent and saved. How does it add up? This task should take ten minutes.

- Check for patterns of spending. Are you spending too much in certain areas? Can you change these habits in the next month or two? This task should take fifteen minutes.

Once a year—

- Gather your financial papers together for taxes. Hopefully, you've kept everything in one folder with all the paperwork for one year. These papers should include tax forms from your bank, mortgage lender, employer, university, etc. This task should take twenty minutes.

- File taxes. This process can take a while if you're doing it by yourself. If you have someone do your taxes, the process can take roughly an hour.

- Organize your tax information and keep the records for seven years. This task should take twenty minutes.

- Review your spending and savings for the last year. Assess how you met your goals and where you can improve for the next year. This task should take up to forty-five minutes.

- Sit down and think about any large expenses you may have coming up in the next year. Do you need to send your child to college, make home improvements, or purchase a new car? This task should take thirty minutes.

- Create a list of debts. Include how much is outstanding and what you'd like to pay each month to pay down these totals. Keep track of your debt to see the progress of paying them off. This task should take up to forty-five minutes.

Conclusion

This chapter included a lot of information about finances. Don't feel obligated to do everything at one time. The best way to ensure that you create long-term practices is to take things slow and steady.

Your financial health can lead to unneeded stress and strain if it is not managed correctly. However, even if you have ADHD, you can come up with a process to help yourself through these tense activities.

CHAPTER TEN

Treatments & Mindset: Rewriting the ADHD Script

Introduction

Although we've given you a host of quick tips throughout the book, there are many other things you can do to help flip the script when dealing with and thinking about your ADHD brain.

ADHD isn't something that defines you. It is part of you, and it can be managed. You can be the manager of your cognitive differences, and you can find out how to do this in the best way for your brain, values, morals, and lifestyle.

Cognitive-behavioral therapy, diet, exercise, and self-care are amazing ways to start. Not everything mentioned in this book will work for you, but some suggestions can work very well. Try another if you find that one thing isn't working for you. You can even take elements from one exercise and combine them with another.

The point of rewriting your script is to reverse the negative self-talk your brain has been telling you for years. This internal dialogue is wrong. You are amazing. Your mind is incredible. You are also creative, intuitive, intelligent, and so much more.

These are the things you will begin telling yourself with the help of the items mentioned above.

Cognitive Behavioral Therapy

Behavioral therapy intervention has shown some incredible results for women with ADHD. Cognitive Behavioral Therapy, or CBT, is a therapy that helps train your brain through a method of medication, talk therapy, and behavioral treatment plans.

Since you may have never attempted any type of treatment when it comes to ADHD, this type of treatment plan may seem overwhelming, but know that once you absorb the information and soak in everything that is needed to help yourself, you're going to get in a groove that works best for you.

Building an ADHD support team with medical and psychological professionals is the top way to help yourself.

Medication

Medical professionals often use stimulant medications as the first line of treatment. However, many women are wary of using medication, but it can help cut through some of the noise in your brain. Depending on your symptoms levels, you may still need other help.

Results of Behavioral Therapy

The positive outcomes of CBT have psychosocial communities encouraged by cognitive-behavioral interventions.

In the article *"Current Status of Cognitive Behavioral Therapy for Adult Attention-Deficit Hyperactivity Disorder,"* the researchers look at several methods, including combined medication and CBT, cognitive-behavioral oriented group rehab, and mindfulness training CBT. These are the methods I encourage you to try when building your therapy strategies.

In combining medication and CBT medication, researchers found a "significant reduction in comorbid anxiety and depression symptoms" for active strategies that combined medicine, learning how to build on your strengths, training coping strategy, and CBT conceptualization and perspective.

With any therapy treatment, you must feel comfortable with what is happening to and in your body. If you are not comfortable taking medication at the onset, that is okay. Follow your instincts. When you listen to what your intuition tells you, you will build confidence in your decision-making skills.

Group rehabilitation with cognitive behavior orientation includes "talk" therapy in a social setting, psychoeducational sessions where you will find out how to help your ADHD, motivational sessions, and initiation on organization, attention, emotional regulation, memory, and communication, self-esteem, and more. This trial found that thirty-one members showed twenty percent improvement in the post-treatment process.

Finally, the mindfulness mediation training addresses mood and anxiety symptoms that tend to saddle ADHD. When this trial was complete, evidence found that thirty percent of participants responded with a decrease in both types of ADHD (inattentive and hyperactivity-impulsivity). Subjects who completed the plan also showed "pre-to-post improvements on a neuropsychological attention conflict and set-shifting."

The purpose of all the information above is to give you an idea of the different types of CBT and some helpful evidence to back up what might work for you.

With CBT, you will embark on a journey that will have you getting to know yourself on a new level. You will work on every aspect of yourself, including knowing when you need to improve upon a feature or when you are too hard on yourself.

Cognitive-behavioral therapy will be a process that runs a marathon, and it isn't a race to get everything in line. You will tackle several things at once, and there will be moments where it doesn't seem like you are getting any movement. Then, one day you'll wake up, and some elements will have clicked into place.

This type of mindfulness intervention builds on layers of good habits and positive self-talk and teaches you how to embrace every part of yourself.

ADHD Diet & Exercise

While you cannot undertake every helpful tip right at once (if you do, you may become overwhelmed and be tempted to give up—don't give up, though! Just take a step back and work on two to three items at a time), there are smaller things you can do to help yourself find a good routine.

Eating clean, whole foods and finding an exercise regime are two nice ways to maintain your ADHD symptoms while working on some of the more heady, complicated things.

Healthy Eating

Although no significant data connects a diet and ADHD, research has discovered indications that certain foods and vitamins may help. For neurology's sake, foods rich in protein like poultry, fish, eggs, nuts, and beans can build the connection between neurotransmitters.

Patients with ADHD who have had a healthy intake of iron, magnesium, and zinc have discovered that their neurotransmitters are regulated, and their cognitive differences level out.

When you incorporate zinc into your diet, it will regulate dopamine, which can calm your brain. Low iron levels will correlate with cognitive issues and have shown spikes in severe ADHD symptoms. Magnesium can be used to have neurotransmitters refocus and relax your brain.

Foods high on the Glycemic Index (GI) can release rapid glucose, increasing inattention, hyperactivity, and impulsivity. Processed foods like artificial dyes and white, refined sugars have a poor connection with brain activity. They are generally recommended to steer clear from when you have any sort of neurological disruption.

If you get knowledgeable about reading the labels on your food packages, you'll be able to learn the foods to stay away from and which ones are good for you. Words like: dehydrated cane juice, dextrin, dextrose, high-fructose corn sweetener, maltodextrin, molasses, malt syrup, and sucrose are all code words for sugar.

Exercise

If you don't like to exercise, it's time to find something that works for you. It can be as simple as an activity like walking. But, with ADHD, exercise is crucial to help focus your brain, burn energy, and relieve yourself of some of those peskier symptoms like impulsivity and inattention.

Even without ADHD, exercise affects the brain positively. Working in a regular exercise routine can play a vital role in brain health by improving memory, enhancing learning capacity, and improving mood.

As we age, our memory functions can decline due to low blood flow to the brain. One of the reasons is that our vascular symptoms begin to stiffen. However, you can counteract this by performing weekly aerobic and anaerobic exercises to improve cardio function.

While enhancing your blood flow, you can also improve your learning. The process of brain plasticity—the ability to change activity due to external and internal stimuli—helps you learn. Exercise is vital in the retention of new physical and mental skills. It is associated with changing how your brain cells communicate with one another.

Exercise also shows a vast improvement in mood. Think about when you get that swift kick of dopamine after indulging in the act of instant gratification. Training can also give you a shot of that feeling, where endorphins and endocannabinoids are released. These chemicals are "feel-good" hormones that let you experience a "high."

Exercise is actually one of the top treatments for both adults and children with ADHD. Going through a weekly exercise regime will promote dopamine release, improve executive function, change brain-derived neurotrophic factor (BDNF) signaling, which is a key factor in how you learn and remember, and impact your attention and behavior.

Some of the best exercises for adults with ADHD are a combination of resistance training and aerobic activity, which can include:

- Bicycling

- Spinning

- Jogging

- Hiking

- Browning

- Elliptical

- Boxing

- Martial arts

- HIIT (high-intensity interval training)

- CrossFit

- Weightlifting

These activities can help prevent mental burnout that can cause inattention and impulsivity when coupled with ADHD.

ADHD & Self-Care

Finally, taking care of yourself will have to be a priority for the foreseeable future. Women have a stigma that they should "fix" everyone and everything else before they can fix themselves. That is the less selfish thing to do, right?

Wrong.

Think about when you are tired and worn. Can you help your children or friends in the way you want to? Instead, you continue to bury yourself in other people's stuff, and before you know it, things just keep coming. If you don't set boundaries and draw the line, nothing else will do it.

You have to be the one who takes control of your life.

You have to be the one who focuses on getting herself better so she can take care of those in her life to the fullest.

Self-care doesn't mean ignoring emergencies or brushing off homework. It can be as simple as taking fifteen minutes of the day to yourself. What you do during these fifteen minutes is entirely up to you.

You can walk, put on a face mask, drink a glass of wine, paint your nails, throw axes at a target, read a book, get your hair cut, eat something delicious, watch a horror movie, and more.

You don't have to indulge in self-care daily. You can do it weekly or monthly. But, you have to make sure to take care of yourself.

When you take care of yourself, you are also a model to your children, friends, and family members to treat themselves with kindness. If they see you accomplish more when you give yourself a little break, they too will realize how good of an idea it is and will engage in self-care.

Final Words

Attention-Deficit Hyperactivity Disorder is a difference in how your brain works from others in the world. ADHD does not need to define you. Instead, let it be your superpower. Discover how you can have your symptoms work with and for you instead of allowing them to run over your life and keep your self-esteem low.

You have issues with ADHD right now because you haven't been given the proper tools to manage it.

This book was created to help you find those tools that will work right with your lifestyle and guide you in the right direction towards helping yourself.

ADHD affects every aspect of your life. You might have stress over relationships, money, and your career. At one point in your life or another (maybe even now), you may have felt as though you were unable to have the career of your choosing, that you were unable to budget your money properly, or that you were never going to find people who could be friends with the real you.

The fact of the matter is that you are incredible.

You have an insanely funny sense of humor. You can think outside of the box. You can multitask. You are intelligent. You are caring, thoughtful, and loving. You have so many good qualities that you aren't even aware of.

Start building your ADHD team today and get to know how truly incredible you are. Start living the life you want to live. The one that you deserve.

Book 2

ADHD Workbook for Women

Proven Exercises & Strategies to Improve Executive
Functioning, Focus and Motivation. Essential Life Skills for
Women with ADHD

Introduction

Hello and welcome:

If you are reading this book, you are probably a person with or have a loved one with ADHD. This book is dedicated to all the women who have gone through most of their lives not realizing they have Attention Deficit Hyperactivity Disorder. If you haven't been formally diagnosed yet, but suspect that you have ADHD, you are not alone.

Most women are not diagnosed until their 30s or early 40s (Sreenivas, S. 24 Mar. 2022. "ADHD in Women."). Many theories of why this happens has to do with the social stigma and the role that we must play in the world.

This workbook will break down some of those theories for you, along with exercises that can challenge ADHD symptoms, encourage you to try new things with ADHD, and help you see the power behind your ADHD. It is also a companion piece to the full book Women with ADHD, which came out in July 2022.

If you are a woman with Attention Deficit Hyperactivity Disorder, chances are you weren't diagnosed until you were an adult. If that is the case, you may have difficulty with organization, chores, career, relationships, friendships, and more.

If you are a mom with ADHD, you may feel inadequate, even though you are not. Many women who are mothers report the same thing. Within these pages, you will get to read some of their confessions and see if it sounds like they share the same thoughts as you do.

Society expects a lot out of a woman.

You expect a lot out of yourself.

If you are a wife and mother, you take care of the lives of your family.

If you are single and career-oriented, you work twice as hard as everyone else to show your worth.

If you are somewhere in between, you still provide incredible value to the world, but it is rarely mentioned.

Women do things because they need to be done, not because they are looking for acclaim, props, and credit—although being appreciated is always nice. There may be times when you don't.

Women with ADHD have a greater inclination toward:

- Depression

- Substance Abuse

- Anxiety

- Eating Disorders

- Mood Disorders

- And More

The tendency to backslide into mental issues doesn't mean something is wrong. It means that you are human.

And humanity isn't something women are supposed to have.

While that may sound dramatic, think about how many times you've made excuses for someone else's behavior. Think about how often you've said "I'm sorry" over something small or when you've had a big emotion you're embarrassed about.

Women aren't supposed to cry or be emotional. We aren't supposed to laugh too loud, talk too much, or emote in a way that makes other people uncomfortable. Women are supposed to be quiet—which is where the ADHD diagnosis comes into play and probably why your diagnosis was missed.

ADHD already has a stigma attached to it. Even with all the research, studies, and evidence found within the last twenty years, people still don't know enough about it. What they do know has been based on gender bias.

Even the DSM-IV for the American Psychological Association (APA) has a foundation of ADHD symptoms rooted in male patients. It wasn't until much later, when there was more information on how ADHD affected people, did women and girls start to be considered to have the disorder?

Perhaps you've just recently been diagnosed. How did you feel about the possibility? Did you scoff or question the professional who labeled you? Did you deny that it could even be a possibility? Was ADHD ever on your radar to begin with? Were you shocked that an adult could be diagnosed with the disorder? Did you have myriad other reactions that all boil down to the simple idea of disbelief?

Any of those reactions are more common than you realize. And being a woman who is diagnosed with ADHD is becoming a natural occurrence.

The first thing you will have to do, even if you're still in denial about your ADHD, is wash your thoughts of everything you know about it. The current stereotype of adolescent boys climbing over the walls and yelling while they cut their hair off with scissors is just that. It's a stereotype. And while stereotypes are grounded in some myopic truth, most of them are misleading on purpose—so no one looks too closely and finds the chinks in society's armor.

The fact of the matter is that anyone anywhere at any time can be affected by ADHD. This statement also means that anyone, anywhere, anytime, can be diagnosed with ADHD.

Women and girls are the most misdiagnosed people of anyone with ADHD. As it stands, ADHD affects about five percent of adults in the United States (Gatti, 2022). Four out of every ten teachers report having difficulty seeing ADHD in their female students as opposed to their male students (Quinn, 2004).

Undiagnosed or untreated ADHD can cause further complications in a person. Women will be misdiagnosed with mood, personality, or other comorbidity (Kessler, 2004).

A rising number of women from age twenty-four to thirty-six are becoming diagnosed with ADHD—they are the fastest growing part of the population to get the diagnosis (Kaleidoscope Society, 2022).

So, are you asking yourself, if professionals know this information, why is it still so hard for a woman or girl to get diagnosed with ADHD? The short answer is that ADHD symptoms show themselves differently in women and girls than in boys and men.

The longer answer is that not much research has been studied about gender and ADHD. The diagnosis has been recorded for over 200 years—under different names, of course. Instead of looking at all the symptoms, researchers have focused on the surface-level ones because they are easier to see.

That information doesn't mean that these researchers haven't done a stellar job figuring out a lot about ADHD. It just means that the disorder is so complex that 200 years+ isn't enough to cover all the ways the condition affects people.

Were there gender biases because boys displayed their symptoms in the open and girls and women internalized them? Yes. But now that scientists have discovered the discrepancy, they are working hard to rectify it.

The average woman with ADHD will have symptoms that look like anxiety, depression, and inattention. Women are far better than men at learning how to mask their issues. Women tend to offset traits they believe are inadequate with other tools that lead them to be labeled "perfectionists." This method, while it sounds great, can be maladaptive and unhealthy. If she continues this way, she will not be able to develop healthy coping skills, and her anxiety will skyrocket.

If you're a woman with ADHD, the first thing you'll need to do is to figure out how its symptoms look on you. Acknowledging your issues and owning up to the possible symptoms will only lead you to a place where you feel at peace and set free.

Once you suspect you have ADHD or get diagnosed, you can learn to develop the tools you need and set yourself up for success. Finding a counselor who has experience with

ADHD is the best step you can take on the road to helping yourself.

How to Use This Book

This workbook will give you information, data, and exercises to help you hone in on your symptoms and find the right tools and routines. The resources at the back of this workbook will give you other avenues to check out.

The exercises in this book are meant to invoke self-reflection, comfort and ease you into new, healthy habits that will manage your ADHD.

When you read through the book, have a notebook and a pen or pencil to write down thoughts or ideas you may have that help. If you've purchased this book in print, you are free to mark it up, but journaling is still encouraged.

At the end of each section, you will find a space where you can write down your thoughts, introspections, and feelings about the information in the chapter. If you don't know where to begin journaling, you can ask yourself a few questions.

1. What did this chapter tell me?

2. Did I learn anything?

3. Do I like anything more than the other ideas in this chapter?

4. Do I want to incorporate an idea into my routine?

5. How can I integrate an idea/s into my practice?

6. What did I feel when reading through this chapter?

7. How can I organize the thoughts in my mind?

8. How does this chapter relate to my ADHD?

9. How can I work with my therapist on these exercises?

10. Do I feel positively or negatively about anything I read?

For question ten, if you find something beneficial or impractical about anything you read, make a note of it. Analyze what about the information that made you feel good, why it made you feel that way, and what you can do about it. If it feels impractical or worthless, you can leave the information in the book and forget about it. However, if the info triggers a distressing reaction, make sure to review it with your therapist.

This workbook is not intended to bring you any tumultuous emotions. Still, anytime you dig into your past and use your feelings while investigating psychological habits, you are bound to have some unpleasantness.

Remember, discomfort and unsavory thoughts mean that you're coming close to unhealthy behavior. These feelings aren't bad, but they are uncomfortable. But if they shift from discomfort to distress, that is a problem you should talk to your therapist about.

The information in this workbook is meant to build a new routine, rewrite the ADHD script, and give you a better outlook on yourself and the world. That doesn't happen without a few bumps and bruises (metaphorical ones), but knowing that you're not alone does make the process much easier.

Pep Talk

You have learned to be resourceful and put others before your progress as a woman. You have adapted to ADHD symptoms and have learned how to mask your issues instead of finding ways to manage them healthily. Yes, you're doing the best you can to survive through the days, but you don't have just to survive. Instead, you can use these exercises and resources to develop helpful, healthy tools that will reroute your ADHD symptoms into a place where you don't feel like you are constantly struggling.

You can release yourself into an easier way of life where you are organized, pay bills on time, and move forward instead of constantly running on a wheel to nowhere.

You are a smart, strong, and intelligent woman.

ADHD does not make you the person you are. It's a neurodivergent development of your brain. It is manageable, and when you learn how to help yourself, you'll see how much more you can help other people, especially those you love.

Although this workbook is a companion piece to the Woman with ADHD book, you'll find exercises that can help you develop new routines, organize your life, and calm the constant chaos inside your chest. You have control over your actions, and by doing the exercises in this book, you're taking control back (or maybe for the first time) and getting the life you want and deserve to live.

However, working through ADHD is not going to be easy. Think about how long you've had the habits ingrained inside of you. It will take time to erase them. Don't worry if you struggle at first. Although it doesn't feel good, the struggle signifies movement and change. Don't worry if things feel uncomfortable—they will. But discomfort isn't a bad thing. It means you're doing things differently than you have in the first place.

You will have days when anxiety and negative self-talk will get better. You will have days where everything falls into place, and you will have more days in between. Even when it seems as though everything is going wrong, tell yourself you're doing it right—because you are doing something to help yourself.

That's all you need.

This book will help you create a solid connection with your ADHD. It will guide you away from bad habits and encourage the acceptance of your entire self.

By looking at the ADHD community of women, you'll find that you're not alone. And if you aren't sure where to start, know I'm right here with you.

We're going to get through this together.

CHAPTER ONE

What is ADHD?

Introduction

Reading this book, you probably already know what ADHD is. However, a brief overview of ADHD can be helpful to refresh your memory and provide a reference if needed.

This chapter will review ADHD and give you some exercises to help you determine what your symptoms are and what type of ADHD you may have. These exercises are in no way a formal diagnosis but a guide to help you find the best treatment plans and solutions to fit your lifestyle.

Throughout this book, you will be reminded that finding professional help from a therapist or psychiatrist who has experience with ADHD is going to be a tremendous asset to you and your plight.

What is ADHD?

ADHD is a neurodevelopmental difference in the way your brain works. People without ADHD, mood disorders, or chemical imbalances have neurotypical brains. Those with ADHD are considered to have neurodivergent brains. When your brain has ADHD, it has not only developed different, but the network of neurons, synapses, and chemicals does not work in the way that a neurotypical brain does—this creates a problem because even though your brain is neurodivergent, any human brain needs certain things to work in a streamlined way.

Instead, your brain is starved of chemicals and hormones like dopamine, the synapse misfires, and the network doesn't run smoothly.

This development creates a lot of issues for those with ADHD, especially if they don't know what is going on.

There are three types of ADHD:

- **Inattentive**—when you have inattentive ADHD, you will have trouble finishing, paying attention, and organizing tasks. Details will also address your issue. You can have problems following conversations or listening to instructions. You probably find that you're easily distracted and even forget about daily routines. This type of ADHD is one of the most common for women, and the quiet nature of the disorder is one of the main reasons girls are not diagnosed in school.

- **Hyperactive/Impulsive**—although it may sound surprising, this type of ADHD is the least common. It is more well-known because the symptoms are louder, larger, and more impulsive. If you have this type of ADHD, you will have trouble sitting still or talking for a long time. You may often react impulsively and feel restless at the same time. You may have loved jumping, climbing, screaming, and running around. Impulsiveness will have you interrupt conversations, grab things, and speak over others. You are probably more prone to accidents and injuries than the average person (Centers for Disease Control and Prevention, 26 Jan. 2021. "What Is ADHD?").

- **Combination**—unsurprisingly, you may realize that the combination type of ADHD is the most common. You could have several symptoms from each category, which makes ADHD unique for each person. (Centers for Disease Control and Prevention, 26 Jan. 2021. "What Is ADHD?").

Exercise One—What Are My Symptoms?

Check off the symptoms that seem to fit your personality and traits. Review the symptoms below to see what type of ADHD matches most with your answers.

- Have problems following through on duties for your job?

- Talk too much.

- Have been accused of not listening during conversations.

- Interrupts other conversations, games, activities, etc., without being asked to join. Alternatively, you may take over an activity completely to avoid having to give instructions or explain yourself.

- Have issues organizing your day—cannot manage time well. You often miss deadlines or have been told your work is disorganized or messy.

- Need to be "on the go" constantly.

- Have an inability to stay seated at work.

- Are unable to do quiet activities.

- Have issues with focus, such as staying on task or finishing activities, especially during conversations, reading, and lectures.

- Dislike or avoid projects that may require continued mental effort, like completing forms and preparing reports.

- Often lose important items that you need daily. Items like cellphones, glasses, keys, wallets, etc.

- You forget daily tasks like chores, errands, keeping appointments, paying bills, and returning phone calls. Have issues sitting still. Often jiggles feet or hands, shifts in your seat, or fidgets.

- You become distracted easily.

- Can't pay attention to details and make careless mistakes at your job.

- You cannot seem to wait for someone to finish asking a question before you complete their sentences or answer. You cannot wait to speak.

(Davis, Sarah, and Linda Hill. 2022. Women with ADHD: The Complete Guide to Stay Organized, Overcome Distractions, and Improve Relationships. Manage Your Emotions, Finances, and Succeed in Life.)

Symptoms

Inattentiveness

- You can't pay attention to details and make careless mistakes at your job.

- Have issues with focus, such as staying on task or finishing activities, especially during conversations, reading, and lectures.

- Have problems following through on duties for your job.

- Have been accused of not listening during conversations.

- Have issues organizing your day—cannot manage time well. You often miss deadlines or have been told your work is disorganized or messy (Psychiatry.org. Accessed Aug. 13, 2022. "What is ADHD?").

- Dislike or avoid projects that may require continued mental effort, like completing forms and preparing reports.

- Often lose important items that you need daily. Items like cellphones, glasses, keys, wallets, etc.

- You become distracted easily.

- You forget daily tasks like chores, errands, keeping appointments, paying bills, and returning phone calls (CDC. Jan. 26, 2021) (Davis, S. 2022).

Hyperactivity or Impulsiveness

- Have issues sitting still. Often jiggles feet or hands, shifts in your seat, or fidgets.

- Have an inability to stay seated at work.

- Need to be "on the go" constantly.

- Talk too much.

- Are unable to do quiet activities.

- You cannot seem to wait for someone to finish asking a question before you complete their sentences or answer. You cannot wait to speak.

- Interrupts other conversations, games, activities, etc., without being asked to join. Alternatively, you may take over the activity completely to avoid having to give instructions or explain yourself (Psychiatry.org. Accessed Aug. 13, 2022.),(CDC. Jan. 26, 2021), (Davis, S. 2022).

When you tally your score, check to see if you have five or more answers. If you do, compare your marks with Inattentive or Hyperactive/Impulsive symptoms. Your responses will give you a better idea of your ADHD type and how to begin to build your treatment plan. When you take your answers to your medical professional, you'll be able to tackle your symptoms one by one.

If you find that you have several from each section—inattentive and hyperactive—you will probably be diagnosed with Combination ADHD and can develop a treatment plan from several angles.

If you have not been formally tested, doing so is a good idea. You'll need to find a therapist or medical professional to perform the test. ADHD is not discovered through blood work. Instead, you'll take a series of paper tests, hearing and vision screenings, and interviews that will take a few days to complete.

Once you are formally diagnosed (or just suspect you have ADHD), you can begin to look at treatments (Davis, S. 2022).

Treatments

Once you realize that you have ADHD, a golden door of opportunities does open up for you. Again, that may sound a little melodramatic, but putting a label on your struggles gives you a map of how to help yourself. When that happens, a weight can be lifted off of your shoulders.

After you've figured out what kind of ADHD type you have, inattentive, hyperactive-impulsive, or combination, you can begin to focus on a plan that will spotlight the most beneficial way to live your best life. You can literally find out how your brain works. It's a pretty cool process.

One caveat, although it happens more often in children transitioning into adulthood, is that sometimes symptoms morph into others. If you start with hyperactivity and find good ways to maneuver your brain in the right way, your brain may overcorrect and shift you into an inattentive form of ADHD. That doesn't mean you can work with those symptoms, but it is something to keep in the back of your mind. This is a possibility (Psychiatry Org, Aug 2022).

This information is meant to discourage you. Instead, think of it as a post-it note reminding you that while ADHD is manageable and you can retrain your brain to create better habits and function properly, it may never go away completely. The human brain can be pretty persnickety in that way, but if you notice some odd diets in your behavior once you've tackled one set of symptoms, you may need to go in and create a few modifications to combat the next type.

Treatment plans usually do include a combination of behavioral therapy and medication. However, your specific play will depend on what your lifestyle requires, what your symptoms are, and where your comfort level lies.

No matter what plan you and the medical professional come up with, it is your plan. You have to be comfortable with it—this statement is different than getting comfortable being uncomfortable. This statement has more to do with your gut. If you don't feel that an aspect of your plan doesn't fit into your beliefs, methods, lifestyle, etc., you need to express it to your therapist.

However, if you believe that you are simply afraid of trying something new, you should also be aware of that. To find out if you are worried or if it is an attack on your core values, you should ask yourself a few questions.

Exercise Two—Developing a Treatment Plan I'm Comfortable With

Think about what your responses would be to the ten questions below. Write out or journal your answers to give you a better idea of what you're comfortable with and what is an absolute non-starter. There is space below to write your answers, or you can do it in a separate notebook.

1.   What am I avoiding?

2.   Am I just afraid of this new process?

3.   Do I think my therapist would steer me in the wrong direction?

4.   Do I trust my therapist?

5.   Do I trust myself?

6.   How can this method help me?

7.   How can this method hurt me?

8.   Am I just not ready to try the process?

9.   Do I not want to try something new because it is unfamiliar to me?

10. Will I be hurting myself (metaphorically) if I don't try it?

_____

_____

_____

_____

_____

_____

_____

_____

_____

_____

_____

_____

_____

_____

_____

_____

_____

_____

_____

_____

_____

_____

_____

_____

_____

_____

_____

_____

_____

_____

_____

_____

_____

_____

_____

So, how do you know if you have a good treatment plan?

A plan that will be beneficial for your ADHD will have you and your therapist monitoring your actions, thoughts, and behaviors closely. You'll have follow-up sessions to discuss what is working and what routines need to be changed. While a therapist is not necessary, finding someone that works with you is an incredibly healthy and helpful resource.

One of the goals of this workbook is to help you manage your systems. However, by going through the book and talking to a therapist, spiritual leader, or another medical professional, you're giving yourself an extra boost of assistance.

The main thing to remember when building your treatment plan is that you're doing this for a better life.

Before developing a treatment plan, you'll have to understand your goals for the program. The next exercise will help you do this.

What are Treatment Goals?

Think about this question. You can develop your treatment goals in several ways. However, because you have ADHD, make sure you use SMART goals. The SMART goal method includes: Specific, Measurable, Attainable, Relevant, and Timely goals (Stewart, Sept. 2021; Main, 2021).

With ADHD, it's good to have a BIG goal in your mind—where you see yourself in three, five, and ten years. But it's equally important, if not more so, to have goals you can break into chunks to complete and accomplish things.

When you incorporate SMART goals into your practice, you're giving yourself smaller goals on your way to working toward bigger goals, and then you can focus on the even larger-scaled goals. You can think of it like stairs, a pyramid, or something else more fun for you. But each time you knock on one of your smaller goals, you've walked up another step.

For your SMART goals, you're going to want to write them down. Most ADHD types do better when they have a visual aid—hence why it is important to have a notebook along with this book. You can use it as a constant reference.

Think about your goals. What is the result you're looking for when managing your ADHD?

An example can be: *I want to have a routine where I wake up every morning, work out, go to my job, come home, clean for twenty minutes, walk the dog, make dinner, and then spend three hours with my family.*

Now, that example is very specific and doesn't have to be that detailed. But it can be. If you don't know what you want your end goal with the ADHD treatment plan to be, that is okay too. You can take it one day at a time.

The sky is limitless to what works best for you.

If you would prefer to know your goal but don't know how to get there—close your eyes and envision who you are and what you are doing in three months, then six, then one year. What does each one of those images look like?

Write it down.

When you have those visions written down, ask yourself where they will lead. Are you looking to become a novelist? Do you want to learn to play the cello? Do you want to run a marathon? Be the president of the PTA?

Once you have a few goals written down, incorporate the SMART method for each one. This method is to help you find short-term success toward your long–term goals.

Exercise Three—What are My Treatment Goals?

Goal: Write down your long-term plan below.

_____

_____

_____

Goals: Break your long-term goal into five short-term goals. Use the SMART Method.

Short-Term Goal

_____

_____

_____

_____

Instructions: Fill out your particular actions below to meet the short-term goal.

Specific—

A specific goal lets you narrow down the idea into one action. You can start with an action word to use in your sentences.

Example: Plan, organize, implement, develop, transform, meditate, run, ride, clean, etc.

Think about these things before or as you are writing:

1. What is your mission?

2. What are the specific terms of the goal? (Steer clear of describing how you will accomplish your goal).

3. Answer Who, What, Where, When, and Why (Stewart, Becca. 23 Sept. 2021).

_____

_____

_____

_____

_____

_____

Measurable—

With your specific goal in mind, explain how you will determine that your particular purpose is complete. What benchmarks do you reach to feel that you've accomplished your plan? Don't be general. Make sure to use as much detail as you can muster up. This goal should be attainable, realistic, and quantitative.

_____

_____

_____

_____

_____

_____

Achievable—

Is your goal realistic? Given your skills, capabilities, level of control, etc., can you reach this goal?

If you find that your goal is to be a pop star, that's a great goal—but it is not a short-term achievable goal until you've already had agents lining up to get your signature on a billion-dollar contract. Instead, you could start by setting your goal toward doing the best you can in public. Alternatively, get three singing gigs for three weekends in a row.

To find out if your goal is achievable, ask yourself the following questions:

1. How heavily does the success of this goal rely on others? Do you only rely on yourself?

2. Do you have time to reach this goal? If not, are you willing to make time?

3. Is the goal possible within the scheduled deadline?

4. Are the parameters too tight or too loose?

5. Will you need help reaching your goal? Who will be the person or people to help you?

6. If you can complete your plan alone, how will you do it?

_____
_____
_____
_____
_____
_____
_____
_____

There is no need to spread yourself too thin in any manner. When people try to accomplish goals, they fail because they have strained themselves physically, mentally, emotionally, and financially.

If you burn out before you reach your goal, you might have a harder time reaching it. Or, the worst-case scenario is that you will give it up. Don't give up if you feel like your dreams are too big or may stretch your abilities right now. Instead, revisit the Specific goal and rewrite it. You can develop something that won't break your bank, spirit, or body (Stewart, Becca. 23 Sept. 2021).

Relevant—

Is your specific goal relevant to your long-term goal?

If you want to be a pop star and your goal right now is to get a car, think about how those two goals connect. Do you want to get a car so you have freedom and independence to go on tour in different cities, or is your goal less connected? It may sound a little weird, but these things matter when planning your short-term goals, especially when you have ADHD (Stewart, Becca. 23 Sept. 2021).

To find out if your goal is relevant to your long-term one, answer the questions below:

1. Does your plan make sense based on what you're already doing?

2. Can you make these changes right now?

3. Does your strategy match the larger purpose of your long-term goals?

4. Does your plan align with your professional and personal values?

If you've answered 'no' to these questions, you should rework your specific goals a little more.

_____

_____

_____

_____

_____

_____

Timely—

Have you given yourself a deadline? If not, make sure to add that to the goal. While you can complete the plan quicker than the scheduled time you set out for yourself, make sure it is a realistic timeframe. Don't put it so close that you cannot achieve it, but don't put it so far away that you don't feel like you need to rush on it.

Usually, a goal of three weeks is an admiral timeline. If you don't think that you can achieve your goal at this time or cannot move things around in your schedule for it—you'll have to look at the plan you set out for yourself and probably rework it a little.

The point of the SMART method is to help you learn how to achieve small-term goals in a realistic amount of time. If you can fit your goal into a timeframe or cannot maneuver it around your schedule, your goal may be too big to be specific.

Write down your deadline. Also, add why it is a realistic timeframe so you understand if it is enough, too much, or just the right amount of time for you (Stewart, Becca. 23 Sept. 2021).

_____
_____
_____
_____
_____
_____
_____

Exercise Four—Acting on My Treatment Goals

Remember that this section concerns your behavioral and medical treatment plans and goals. When you act on those goals, you will need some tools to help keep you motivated. This next exercise will give tips to help you follow through with your goals and help you hold yourself accountable when you do not.

- **Write down your goals.** An article in Psychology Today discussed how writing your goals down can achieve thirty-three percent higher culpability. In the article, Marilyn Price-Mitchell also discovered:

"Research has uncovered many key aspects of goal-setting theory and its link to success (Kleingeld et al., 2011). Setting goals is linked with self-confidence, motivation, and autonomy (Locke & Lathan, 2006)."

When you write down your goals, keep them in a familiar area so you can look at them often and be reminded of them. If you have any ADHD, this tip is a helpful one to keep the goals at the forefront of your mind.

- **Share your ideas and goals with your family or friends**. Many people are a little gun-shy about this particular tip. Sharing your thoughts with others can leave you feeling open to vulnerability. However, when you share parts of yourself with the people who love and care about you, they should support it. They may even help you figure out how to do things better.

- **Visualize your results**. Professionals, especially athletes and performers, use visualization to walk through the motions of them doing their job flawlessly. Through this vision, they will also reach their ideal outcome (basketball players want to get the ball in the net, singers want to put on a dynamite show). A vision board is a great way to make your goals real.

If you are not ready to create a vision board (more on this later), you can close your eyes and see yourself completing your desired result.

- **Revisit your goals—a lot**. Make sure to check in with your goals frequently. Once you do this, you can track your progress and see where there may need to be some changes. As you grow and develop your treatment plan, what was important to you may no longer grow to be. However, that does not mean you stop wanting things, and it does not mean that you should stop making goals. Change things as needed, and you will find that your goals are still achievable.

Examples of Treatment Goals

If you are still having trouble coming up with goals for your treatment, read the list below to see if there is something familiar you can take and use until you get into the habit of forming goals. Below is a list of example goals, some space to do some writing, or make sure to use your notebook to brainstorm your thoughts after you read the sample goals (Stewart, Becca. 23 Sept. 2021).

- Learn to be less distracted by the voices and music when I am in public.

- Learn how to accept myself.

- Learn how to discuss my ADHD struggles confidently.

- Create an exercise regime.

- Find out more about ADHD

- Find out more about my hormones

- How do I motivate my mind when I am distracted?

- Discover more about Executive Function and how I can improve it.

- Learn about Object Permanence and how it applies to ADHD.

- How can I organize my home to fit with my ADHD?

- Schedule work and processing time.

- Enlist people who love and care about me to help.

- Learn more about ADHD and social habits.

- Learn more about ADHD and my sex life.

- Find out how to be more compassionate with my children.

- Discover how to use mindfulness in my ADHD routines.

Healthy Living

One of the best ways to begin your ADHD treatment plan is to get into a healthy mindset. Think about how you treat your body. What kinds of food do you eat? Do you exercise? How do you sleep? What activities do you enjoy doing? Regardless of your neurological makeup, when you treat your body healthily and respectfully, it works better. Clean food and five hours a week of activity will help release beneficial chemicals into your brain to help it work with less stuttering. While we will discuss healthier living in a later chapter, below are some quick tips to get you started.

- **Discover a healthier way to eat:** look at your eating habits—are they good, moderate, bad, or unhealthy? The only person you have to be honest with yourself about this is you. You know if there are times when you binge eat a package of Oreos or if you mostly eat clean foods and whole grains. You know. Nevertheless, when you eat bad stuff, even if it tastes incredible, that moment of blissful eating only lasts a short while.

Processed foods, white bread, and refined sugars affect your body differently. If you do not think so, make sure you start to keep a food diary of how you feel after you eat healthily versus how you feel if you eat garbage food.

You will not be able to switch all your bad habits at once. And no one is asking you to; however, if you take small steps toward eating healthy—such as finding one healthy food that you enjoy eating or finding recipes that might be good—then you are making progress. You are not doing this to lose weight; you are doing it to help your body work better.

- **Make time for three to five hours of weekly exercise or physical activity.** Find activities you like and want to do. Once you get into a good workout, change your routine so you do not get bored.

One hour a day is a fantastic way to burn up some excess ADHD energy and keep you going in the long run.

As you work out, you will feel better because endorphins and cortisol are released more frequently into your system. These are great chemicals that help your body work at its highest capacity. The more you engage in physical fitness, the better tuned in you are going to be. The more tuned in you get with it, the more you will be able to manage your ADHD.

- **Find out about sleeping better.** Different age groups need different amounts of sleep—however, studies have found that sleep gives your body and mind the time it needs to rest. It also cleanses your body of toxins your brain picks up throughout the day, and several areas of your brain will change their activity level between sleeping and waking.

In these times, your molecular mechanisms will clear away a lot of gathered dirt and debris that will slow your brain down and will replenish your brain with cleaner, newer chemicals like melatonin, GABA, adenosine, and more (Healthy Sleep. Harvard Med. Accessed 14, Aug. 2022. "Why Do We Sleep, Anyway?), (National Institute of Neurological Disorders and Stroke. Accessed 14 Aug. 2022. "Brain Basics: Understanding Sleep), (Davis, S. 2022.)

- **Watch your screen time.** Careers that work with computers may make using this tip a little more tricky than it can seem at first glance. We are all told to keep our screen time low, but it is hard to do with e-books, phones, tablets, and laptops.

If you find it difficult to start with this tip, just stay away from a screen for one hour before you go to bed to see how your sleep works.

To keep yourself from checking your phone, put it away at night before lying down. You can do this by putting it on a charging station that is not in your bedroom or farther away from your bed.

If that does not work, try to take short breaks each hour to give your brain, eyes, and body a rest from screens.

Conclusion

Attention Deficit Hyperactivity Disorder has some unique traits and hurdles to jump over, but with practice, determination, and kindness for yourself, you'll be able to get through anything.

Chapter Two

Women & ADHD

Introduction

In the companion book Women with ADHD (Davis and Hill, 2022), there is a discussion about how to accept your diagnosis. Whether at first, you may think that the doctor is wrong or that a veil to a deeper part of yourself has been lifted, your process will begin with acceptance.

First, you'll have to do a few things:

- **Accept**—Your brain chemistry doesn't mean there is anything wrong, broken, or bad with how your brain works.

- **Accept**—ADHD does not define you. ADHD is part of your identity, but it is not the only thing.

- **Accept**—Even without ADHD, life will continue to have its ups and downs. Now, with practice, routine, and solutions, you may be able to manage those rollercoaster moments a little bit more.

- **Accept**—you will still get stressed. ADHD will still get in the way, but how you talk about it can help you flip your feelings around.

Exercise Five: Learning About Your Acceptance and Denial

This exercise will flex your ability to reframe the dialogue you have with yourself. Inner dialogue can be incredibly invasive and can lead you down a rabbit hole of dissatisfaction and untruths about yourself.

What would you say if you took a step away from the negative self-talk in your head and instead talked to and about yourself as you would if you were speaking to a friend? How would you give this advice?

If you call yourself dumb, stupid, or an idiot—or allude to it from an action you make. For example, if you made a simple mistake by misplacing your keys and muttering, "I'm such an idiot," to yourself. Would you tell your friend they are an idiot if they lost their keys, or would you tell them that it happens to everyone?

Instructions:

1. Write down actions that have occurred.

2. Include what you THINK about yourself when it happens.

3. Be as brutal as your mind is.

Don't do this to be mean to yourself, but to see how wonky your brain works. When you visualize the words you say to yourself, you will see how unforgiving you are about ADHD.

Underneath the unforgiving statement, write a different phrase about the same experience, only this time, pretend you are speaking to a friend. Do you see how you talk to yourself differently than speak to others? Once you know the difference, it will be time to give a more positive, forgiving, and reframed statement to yourself about your ADHD and actions that may relate to your diagnosis.

1. What Happened?

_____

_____

What did your inner dialogue say?

_____

_____

_____

What would you say to a friend?

_____

_____

_____

2. What Happened?

_____

_____

What did your inner dialogue say?

_____

_____

_____

What would you say to a friend?

_____

_____

_____

3. What Happened?

_____

_____

What did your inner dialogue say?

_____

_____

_____

_____

What would you say to a friend?

_____

_____

_____

4. What Happened?

_____

_____

What did your inner dialogue say?

_____

_____

_____

What would you say to a friend?

_____

_____

_____

5. What Happened?

_____

_____

What did your inner dialogue say?

_____

_____

_____

_____

What would you say to a friend?

_____

_____

_____

Once you get into good practice with reframing, you'll find it easier to forgive yourself for little mistakes, and your negative self-dialogue will shift into a more positive light.

Nikki Kinzer, a certified ADHD coach and podcast host from the organization _Take Control of ADHD_, says:

"Before you can fully accept your ADHD, it's important to understand your ADHD. Many clients are surprised when I tell them it's not them; it's ADHD. It's very difficult to separate what's ADHD and what's not. The more you learn about it, the better (Kinzer, 2022)."

The key takeaways Kinzer encourages are:

- You are not broken.

- You do not need to be fixed.

- It's a process to shed the shame and stigma around ADHD; there are a lot of misconceptions of what it is and isn't, but think about how it would feel to accept yourself regardless of how the ADHD shows up (Kinzer, 2022).

Why Didn't Anyone Know?

You may ask yourself, why didn't anyone know or suspect your ADHD before you became diagnosed?

There are a few reasons:

- First, ADHD tests have synonymously been male-forward. Only over the past twenty years have girls been included in trials, research, and studies. DSM-V still only has symptoms that relate to male test subjects instead of using the more inclusive signs found in all genders (Sarkis, 2011).

- Next, women and girls can be misdiagnosed. Because ADHD presents itself differently in females than in males, ADHD can be diagnosed as anything from depression to bipolar (ADDitude Editors and Littman, 2022; Low and Lakhan, 2022).

- Researchers at the National Libraries of Medicine (NIH) conducted a study on "Females with ADHD." They developed a theory called "the female protective effect," This theory surmises that women (and girls) have a higher threshold of external stimuli for their ADHD to come out (Young et al., 2020; Taylor et al., 2016; Davis et al., 2022).

Sarah Ludwig Rausch, a journalist, ADHD advocate, and woman with ADHD, shares her experience before and after her diagnosis in her article, "So That's Why I Found My Phone in the Fridge Again (2022)!"

Rauch dictates her discovery not because she had problems in her life but because she noticed that a reader of her work listed the symptoms that led the reader to get tested for ADHD. When Rauch read about the reader's symptoms, she stated, "It was like I was reading about my own life (Rausch)." Her article details a list of things that seem like innocent mistakes, but when stacked up daily, they can lead to stress, frustration, and poor life management.

"Late for everything? Check.

Always losing your phone/keys/other important items? Check.

Difficulty focusing? Constantly putting off work that takes a lot of concentration? Completely disorganized despite your best efforts?

Check, check, and check (Rausch)."

Many women with ADHD feel that something is missing; if they could just figure out what it is, everything else would fall into place. While getting your ADHD diagnosis can be the missing key, rewriting the ADHD script will be a little harder than sliding a key into a lock and turning. Instead, you will have to unwind each part of your ADHD and start at the beginning. Discover what the triggers are and where your barriers lie. To do that, you will become more self-reflective and learn to get comfortable with some uncomfortable situations.

Breaking the Barriers of ADHD

The previous statement about getting comfortable with uncomfortable situations does not mean that you (or we) will be putting yourself in harm's way. It means that you will have some discomfort through self-reflection and redirecting habits because the new practices are something you have not done before.

Think about a friend (or yourself) who has "tried" something for a few days or even weeks, but they eventually give it up because "it did not work for them" or "they did not like it." Unfortunately, there is a high possibility that they just were not comfortable with the process. The other option is that they really didn't like the experience, which is a fine line you will also have to figure out. It's important to listen to your instincts, but pushing against barriers you've built up for yourself to protect your mind and emotions from ADHD symptoms is equally important.

For example, you do not like watching sports. You especially don't like watching them on television. If you are at a stadium, you would much rather be walking around looking at things than sitting there watching people perform feats of strength against each other while a mascot tries to get me to pander to them along with the rest of the crowd. No amount of rewriting your ADHD brain will make you like sports—this type of entertainment just isn't for you.

If you have moments where your emotions spike because they get triggered by losing keys and being late to take my son to baseball practice, where you wind up snapping at him because you hate sports, that is something you can rewrite. First, it is not your son's fault that you do not like sports, lose your keys, or are overwhelmed by having to take him to practice when nothing is going right. Honestly? It is not your fault, either.

Your ADHD symptoms have been how you have functioned for most of your life, if not your whole life. It can't be unwritten with the click of your fingers.

Think about the several things that can be rewritten in the latter example of getting overwhelmed. Before you think that there is no way to do it, remember that there is always a way to build healthier habits for a more organized lifestyle.

The first step that you will have to take is to discover how your ADHD symptoms affect your daily life. Then you will have to come up with a plan so you can begin to rework, rewrite, and reflect on how you look at ADHD, daily tasks, bigger projects, and more.

Exercise Six: What Everyday Stressors Are ADHD Symptoms

List your daily actions below. Anything you question about yourself, like "Why cannot I {insert chosen responsibility, example, issue, etc.}?" or "Why don't I {insert chosen responsibility, example, issue, etc.}?"

Chances are, if you try your damndest to get something situated but still cannot manage to do so, it is probably part of your ADHD. See examples below for a better idea of tackling this exercise. The purpose of getting your symptoms down and out is to realize and recognize how your brain sometimes works against you, despite how often and hard you try. When you recognize your symptoms are separate from your person, it is much easier to view things with kindness and come up with the best plan of action to shift gears.

Examples:

- I always forget where I put my keys—even if I try to put them in a designated area.

- I set my alarm so I could show up to work on time, but I still managed to be twenty minutes late.

- Even with a list for the grocery store, I find so many interesting items. I always go way over my budget.

Your Turn:

- _____
- _____
- _____
- _____
- _____
- _____
- _____
- _____
- _____
- _____
- _____
- _____
- _____
- _____
- _____
- _____
- _____

Once you complete this exercise, sit down and reflect on what your ADHD symptoms are. If you see a pattern or habit, you can start to build a plan that will help you correct or redirect the issue.

Exercise Six: Mindfulness Breathing

Mindfulness breathing can help you with many things, especially stress, anxiety, and big emotions caused by traumatizing moments. This type of thinking, breathing, and other exercises will be discussed throughout the workbook. Mindfulness breathing can also help you start to recognize where, when, and why your ADHD symptoms appear.

Mindful breathing is a practice you can do anytime, anywhere. When you use this breathing regularly, your stress levels lower, your thoughts will be clearer, and you will have an overall sense of calmness (Celestine, 2022).

Mindful breathing will give you a gentle focus on your breath. Pay attention to the air coming in and out of your nose and mouth. Do not try to change your breathing. You have no expectations about how to do it. Instead, you are simply aware of your breath from moment to moment.

Even if you do not realize it, when you breathe with mindful intentions, you are in a state of meditation. Other meditative practices involve concentration at the present moment. This consideration will include what you are thinking, feeling, and sensing right as you breathe in and out.

You will not judge thoughts, feelings, senses, or actions in this practice. You will just be.

Deep breathing exercises link the benefits of deep breathing to mindfulness to help you cope better with stressful or triggering times.

Instructions: Practice this exercise when you wake up before you go to bed or whenever you begin to feel anxious, stressed, or targeted for rejection. To apply mindful breathing to your routine, do the following:

1. From your seated or standing position, inhale on the count of four.

2. Hold your breath for the count of three.

3. Exhale on the count of four.

4. Repeat five to ten times.

If you prefer a different position or perspective, try the exercise below in the morning after you wake up or just before you go to bed.

- Stand up straight, then bend at the waist.

- Dangle your arms close to the floor.

- Inhale slowly for a count of three.

- Return to a standing position by rolling up slowly. Lift your head last.

- Hold your breath for a count of four.

- Exhale your breath for a count of five.

- As you exhale, slowly bend over again with your hands above your head and dangling at the side of your arms.

- Repeat for three cycles.

- Reflect on how you feel afterward—pay attention to your mind, body, and emotions (Celestine, 2022).

By working on mindfulness breathing in these moments, you are teaching your brain to behave differently.

This workbook will touch on mindfulness exercises more in later chapters. However, if you are interested in looking up other types of mindfulness, read the list below. The practices below can be structured or unstructured:

- Pay attention.

- Accept yourself.

- Live in the moment.

- Bring your focus to your breathing.

- Sitting meditation.

- Meditative walking.

- Body scan meditation (Mayo Clinic Staff, 2020).

When you are asked to **pay attention**, it may seem like a simple request. However, this practice takes focus. It also requires you to slow down your brain, body, and emotions to meet the moment. Paying attention will have you participate right where you are at. You will engage all senses—sight, smell, sound, taste, and touch—as they happen. This exercise will not have you experiencing something on a grand scale. For example, if you are watching a baseball game, instead of watching the entire game, take time to notice what the pitcher is doing, what actions the second-base player is doing, how the grass looks on the field, and what the stadium around you sounds like, etc. (Mayo Clinic Staff, 2020).

While a baseball game may be a grand example, the point of the exercise will be to remove yourself from the event and observe the action. Your goal would be to focus on one thing at a time and give yourself that one thing full attention.

This type of mindfulness will help you retrain your brain into a different way of focusing.

Accepting yourself can be a difficult task to master, and even if you have finally accepted yourself for who you are, you will find that there will be days when you still aren't as kind as you could be.

However, each time you recognize that you are engaging in negative self-talk or self-deprecation, ask yourself, "Would I say this to anyone else?" And instead, think of how you would talk to your friend if they went through or experienced the same thing—don't think about what you should have said or could have done. Accept that the moment happened as it did, and the only thing you can do about it is to learn from it. Before learning from it, you must be nice to yourself, talk to yourself as if you are your best friend, and remind her that it is okay to make mistakes. For example, if you went to a baseball game because you thought it would be fun, then realized that you hate baseball, what would you say to yourself?

To **live in the moment** is similar to paying attention. However, with this mindfulness practice, you will find enjoyment at the moment you are paying attention to (Mayo Clinic Staff, 2020). If, for example, you're back at that baseball game and the sun is warm and shining on you, soak in the warmth. Instead, savor the snack in a way you have not before if you are eating a box of popcorn.

Exercise Seven: Examples of Living in the Moment (LITM)

Instructions: Think about ten things that you really enjoy. Write down why you enjoy them and how they make you feel. Then, when you get a chance, do one of those things. Make sure to pay attention to what is going on and live in the moment—you can even come back to the book and write down how your experience changed.

Example Moment: I really like to read books.

Explanation LITM: When I read, I am at my own time and pace. I connect to myself in a way I do not normally. I love the feeling of turning pages like I am accomplishing something. If I am lying in bed, the blankets are cozy, and the pillow cushions my head. I remind myself to inhale and exhale during quiet moments of the story and realize I am holding my breath during a tenser moment.

1.   Moment One:

_____

_____

Explanation LITM:

_____

_____

2.   Moment One:

_____

_____

Explanation LITM:

_____

_____

3.   Moment One:

_____

_____

Explanation LITM:

_____

_____

4.   Moment One:

_____

_____

Explanation LITM:

_____

_____

5.   Moment One:

_____

_____

Explanation LITM:

_____

_____

6.   Moment One:

_____

_____

Explanation LITM:

_____

_____

7.   Moment One:

_____

_____

Explanation LITM:

_____

_____

8.   Moment One:

_____

_____

Explanation LITM:

_____

_____

9.   Moment One:

_____

_____

Explanation LITM:

_____

_____

10.   Moment One:

_____

_____

Explanation LITM:

_____

_____

After you get into a good habit of living in the moment, you can make it a planned experience or discover that it begins to happen spontaneously. Make sure to remind yourself to do it every once in a while. It is a great way just to reset yourself when you need to.

If you are looking to delve into deeper meditation types that are still easy to do, even while you are working, try some of the below meditative mindfulness exercises to see if you would like to look into them even further.

Sitting meditation will have you sit in a chair. While you should have quiet time, you can be at work and take a five-minute break to engage in your meditative state. Sit with your back straight, feet flat on the ground, and hands in your lap. The most important part of this position is to make sure you are comfortable. You will not want to move. Instead, you will focus on breathing. You will move your breath in and out of your body. When your thoughts or physical feelings interrupt your focus, note them, but bring your attention back to your breath.

Walking meditation is a good thing to try on a lunch or midday break. When you try walking meditation, you will look for a quiet place roughly twenty feet long. Then, you will walk slowly back and forth between these spots. Instead of noticing the sounds, people, and cars around you, focus on your walking. Pay attention to your subtle movements, how your body keeps balance, and be aware of how much energy it takes just for you to stand upright. This practice is good for about ten to fifteen minutes but can be shorter if you just need to get away from the desk for a few moments.

For **body scan meditation,** the best practice is to lie on your back with your arms and legs spread out to your sides. Make sure your palms are facing up. If you want to scan your body and you are at work, sitting is fine as well—you can turn your palms up in your lap if you need a few minutes to try this.

Once you are comfortable, you will close your eyes and bring all your focus to your toes. Then the pad of your foot, then your heel, and move up to your ankle, calves, knees, etc. Keep moving up your body in small increments (Mayo Clinic Staff, 2020). Make sure to touch every part of your body that you can recall and do it systematically. Essentially, you will be running a scan of your body.

Each time you touch a new area, bring your sensations, emotions, and thoughts to the forefront. Each part may incur new senses and bring about new revelations.

You can practice any of the above exercises whenever the mood strikes you or you can carve out some time to work on them. The more you use mindfulness exercises, the easier they will settle into your routine. Evidence from studies has found that anyone can benefit from engaging senses when they are outdoors (Mayo Clinic Staff, 2020).

Trying different mindfulness exercises daily for six months will help you have an effortless transition into using the practices when you need them. You can make a commitment to nurture and reconnect with yourself and you will have an amazing set of tools to help you with ADHD symptoms, stress, and other experiences (Mayo Clinic Staff, 2020).

Conclusion

Learning how your ADHD symptoms affect your daily life will help you move toward a more organized mind, which will trickle down into everything else in your world.

The next chapter will discuss the executive function and give you an idea of how to build up better skills to develop growth and manage your ADHD a little more.

CHAPTER THREE

Executive Function & ADHD

Introduction

Being a woman with ADHD comes with a unique set of challenges that have not been fully studied yet. However, one thing that is incredibly common with ADHD is that executive function skill sets are not fully developed—up to 90% of kids who are diagnosed with ADHD also have issues with executive functions.

Executive function skills help establish structures and strategies for managing projects and determine the actions required to move each project forward (Davis & Hill, 2022). This skill set was supposed to develop fully in childhood, alongside certain fine and gross motor skills. However, when your brain has ADHD, the cognitive process that organizes your activities and thoughts, prioritizes tasks, makes decisions, and manages time efficiently does not develop correctly.

This undeveloped part of the brain happens due to an inability of your neurons to speak to one another as they would if your brain were neurotypical.

Executive Function and ADHD

Executive functions establish follow through and strategy building with projects, complete things on a deadline, and more. When there is executive dysfunction, you struggle to plan, organize, schedule, complete tasks, and analyze important things. You would also have issues keeping track of materials and prioritizing and tend to get overwhelmed by big projects (Barkley & Novotni, 2022).

If this sounds like an issue you are having with ADHD, this chapter will help you pinpoint some of the more troublesome issues and give you some tips on how to begin to build a better structure of executive skills.

Some people with ADHD have issues with executive function because these skills form in the prefrontal cortex, where most ADHD issues also occur. These neurodivergent traits happen because there is a lack of chemicals needed for the brain to communicate in a neurotypical way.

Although up to 90% of those diagnosed with ADHD have executive function issues, not everyone with executive function issues may have ADHD (at least, not that has been discovered as of the writing of this workbook).

You will be able to see the links below between executive function and the neurodivergent way your ADHD works. There are four "circuits" that connect certain parts of your brain. When these circuits do not function properly, there is a lack of communication—this creates issues with time management, goal setting, and more.

The four circuits are as follows:

The Who—this is a circuit that travels from the frontal lobe to the back hemisphere of your brain. It is where self-awareness happens, which is how you know what you are externally and internally feeling, how you know what you do, and what is happening to you.

The What—is a circuit that connects the frontal lobe to the basal ganglia, specifically, the striatum. This part of your brain is linked to memory and is attached to how we think and do. This circuit is important for plans, goals, and the future.

The Why—is a circuit that bridges the frontal lobe and the central brain, or the anterior cingulate, to the amygdala. The amygdala opens to the limbic system, which is linked to your emotions and joins together how you think and feel. In this circuit, your thoughts will invoke your feelings, and your feelings will invoke your thoughts.

The "why" circuit determines the final marker of your plans. If you think about multiple things at a time, this part of your brain will choose the option that best suits the moment, motivation, and emotional properties that match your feelings.

The When—this circuit will travel from the prefrontal area back to the cerebellum. This part of your brain is the backmost area, which coordinates the sequence of actions and the timeliness of when you get certain things done. If you have issues with time management, your "when" circuit is working improperly.

As you see the connection between synapse miscommunication and the ability of the core circuits to work together, you will see how they connect with ADHD. When these circuits miscommunicate, they will affect the main skills driven by executive function (Barkley & Novotni, 2022). These skills are described in the article "What is Executive Function? 7 Deficits Tied to ADHD" by Dr. Russell Barkely. Barkley says that the seven deficits that are tied to ADHD are:

1. **Self-awareness**—attention directed at yourself by you.

2. **Inhibition**—controlling your actions and not indulging in every thought or idea.

3. **Non-verbal working memory**—the ability to hold visual images in your mind and describe how well you can picture things.

4. **Verbal working memory**—inner dialogue.

5. **Emotional self-regulation**—using the first four executive functions to help you process and alter feelings toward specific events.

6. **Self-motivation**—motivation when there is no immediate outside consequence. How often do you finish something when you have nothing to lose or gain?

7. **Planning and problem solving**—how you play with information to come up with things, especially if there is a snag or snarl. This skill shows that there is always another way of doing things (Barkley & Novotni, 2022).

These functions should develop over time and tend to do so chronologically. In people with neurotypical brains, self-awareness develops by age two, and by age thirty, executive function skill sets should be fully formed. Those with neurodivergent brains and diagnosed with ADHD are roughly forty percent behind their peers when developing one function to the next.

Because this happens, children and adults with ADHD have had trouble dealing with relevant age situations and tend to act and think like those from a younger age bracket.

Exercise Eight: Testing your Adult Executive Function Skills

Executive dysfunction can certainly create struggles in every aspect of your life. You may have challenges completing, organizing, scheduling, and planning tasks. You may also have issues balancing tasks, recalling what needs to be done, making multi-step directions, staying on track, holding yourself accountable, and finishing tasks.

Below is a self-diagnosis test that will help you know if you have signs of executive dysfunctions—this is not a formal diagnosis. You can take this test to show your medical professional where you are and they can work out a treatment plan to strengthen your skillset.

How quickly do you let go of your anger as easily as it came on?

- Very Often
- Rarely
- Often
- Never
- Sometimes

How often do you tell yourself, "I will do it later," and then forget about it completely?

- Very Often
- Rarely
- Often
- Never
- Sometimes

How often do you become absorbed in projects that interest you to the detriment of other obligations and even people?

- Very Often
- Rarely
- Often
- Never
- Sometimes

How frequently do you forget important things, even those important to you?

- Very Often
- Often
- Sometimes

- Rarely
- Never

How quickly do you become frustrated when things do not go to plan? Does your frustration follow up with anger?

- Very Often
- Often
- Sometimes

- Rarely
- Never

How often do you become distracted by things you hear or see?

- Very Often
- Often
- Sometimes

- Rarely
- Never

Do you often lose interest in tasks quickly, even when you start with enthusiasm?

- Very Often
- Often
- Sometimes

- Rarely
- Never

How messy is your personal space? Do you frequently struggle with clutter?

- Very Often
- Often
- Sometimes

- Rarely
- Never

How difficult is it for you to move from one task to another and complete a task?

- Very Difficult
- Often Difficult
- Sometimes Difficult
- Rarely
- Never

Do you have issues knowing where to start on a project? Can you prioritize the items in a list?

- Very Often
- Often
- Sometimes
- Rarely
- Never

How frequently do you have problems starting or initiating tasks?

- Very Often
- Often
- Sometimes
- Rarely
- Never

How often do you misplace or lose items? For example, wallet, cellphone, glasses, keys, etc.?

- Very Often
- Often
- Sometimes
- Rarely
- Never

How hard is it for you to follow conversations due to distractions or remember what you wanted to say?

- Very Often
- Often
- Sometimes
- Rarely

- Never

Can you start or do things when the activity does not highly stimulate you?

- Very Often
- Rarely
- Often
- Never
- Sometimes

How often do you forget an appointment or are late for an event?

- Very Often
- Rarely
- Often
- Never
- Sometimes

Have you wasted time trying to choose what to do first in an event, activity, or project?

- Very Often
- Rarely
- Often
- Never
- Sometimes

(Bailey & Panel, 2022)

Look at your answers to the questionnaire above. Does that sound like you? Did you answer most of the questions as "sometimes, often, or very often?" Do you struggle with knowing how to help yourself and figuring out what steps to take to help build your executive function skills? The exercise below can help you with those. Also, find some simple strategies to set you on the right path.

Although there are many ways to reinforce executive function skills, below is a quick overview of strategies that can help you know where to start. Effective strategies can help you when facing challenges and will bolster your methods with healthy tools.

General Strategies

- Chunk your projects into small sub-tasks.

- Use visual organizational tools. For example, whiteboards, virtual calendars, phone notifications, etc.

- Use time organizers like watches, alarms, timers, etc.

- Ask for both written and oral directions when you are able.

- Use a visual schedule and continue to check it throughout the day (set reminders to do so).

- Plan for a time between tasks to transition from one project to another.

Manage Your Time

- Use a to-do list and estimate how long each task will take.

- Use the chunk method for all projects and assign deadlines for completing each chunk.

- Use your visual schedule to track due dates, chores, activities, and long-term projects.

- Use virtual calendars or apps to help manage your schedule and daily calendars or planners to write the same information.

- Tag each assignment with a deadline (no matter how small it seems).

Space and Material

- Purchase decorative and colorful organizers to clean up your workspace.

- Keep important objects that you will use daily or weekly in your line of view or clear containers so you will not forget about them.

- Put anything away that you will not or have not used in the last month. Add them to storage containers with lids.

- Throw away any clutter that is not a bill or important piece of paper. Clear your desk of everything but a few tools.

- Separate workspaces. Keep work stuff in one area, bills in another, etc.

- Schedule a time to organize and clean your workspace each week.

At work

- Create a checklist for assignments. For example:

- Put the due date on the project.

- Reread directions.

- Follow up with my manager.

- Troubleshoot problems.

- List any new issues.

- Close out the project for the day.

(LD Online Writing Staff, n.d.)

While some of these items may sound as though they are simple or even maybe repetitive to what you have heard in the past, do not knock them until you try them. If you have tried them already, try them one more time. You do not know what will stick with you now as opposed to what place you were in previously.

Although you do have to find the right strategy for how your mind works and how your habits will form, make sure to try processes for 21 days or longer before you give up doing them. Also, remember that things will be easier to do at first, then will feel more difficult, and you will want to quit, but keep moving. Dig your heels in if you have to, you are worth putting in the effort for. You deserve to live a life with a little less clutter and chaos. And the methods above may just be a gateway for doing them.

Exercise Nine: Practice Builds Skills

Executive function skills are a mental toolkit for success (Hendry et al., 2016). And although Hendry and his colleagues discussed the idea of toddlers developing these skills, if your executive functions are latent or were not developed, you incur more frustration than you need. While executive function is predictive of career or academic success, know that it has nothing to do with how smart you are (Alloway & Alloway, 2010).

Building these skills will not take much more than a little determination and commitment. Also, note that the less you impair your executive functions with things like stress or strain, you will be able to help them flourish, which is another reason to be kind to yourself (Diamond, 2022).

The activities below will focus on three core executive functions. These skills will be

1. Inhibitory Control.

2. Working Memory.

3. Cognitive Flexibility.

Inhibitory control can be seen in examples like resisting temptations, curbing impulsivity, and thinking before taking action or speaking. Situations like staying on task no matter how bored you require inhibitory control

Some activities that can help you improve inhibitory control are below:

- Play Simon Says—it sounds silly and can be, but when you have a friend, partner, or child, be Simon and follow their instructions. You can have a great time while building up some new skills.

- Go to an acting class. Perform comedy or drama scenes to build inhibitions through other characters.

- Play music with other people in your house. Everyone gets to listen to one song, and you must wait your turn to do it.

- <u>Tag team listening</u>. Take turns with a partner or friend by reading something or listening to the other person read. This practice will strengthen your communication skills by having to listen instead of speaking over others (Diamond, 2022).

- <u>Listen to stories</u>. Using audiobooks as tools will allow you to concentrate on what is being said without visual aids. Sustained auditory attention with a story will strengthen your focus and attention control.

- <u>Learning balance</u>. Balance is all about focusing on one thing to meet a specific goal. Some balanced activities can be:

  o *Walking on any line*—this can be straight or curved. If you find that it is too easy to follow the line, put something in your hand or on your head to level the task up.

  o *Use a bell when you walk*—hold a bell and walk without making a noise. This activity is good to use when you need to calm down.

  o *Find a log*—just like walking on a line, using a log will force focus, or you will fall. Be careful not to hurt yourself, and do not walk on a log over a gorge or high from the ground. Keep your logs to ones that have already fallen and are fully grounded.

- <u>Use crafts to</u> build concentration and reduce clumsiness. Beading or braiding work well for both of these.

When using **working memory**, your brain will absorb and hold information in your mind. It will then process the information to play or work with it. If your mind does not manipulate it that way, the data will be stored in short-term memory and quickly forgotten.

Although both are important, working memory and short-term memory use information differently. Working memory will allow you to:

- Engage in self-reflection.

- Consider the future.

- Reflect on past instances.

- Mentally play with ideas and relate them to others.

- Use multi-layered instructions and follow them in the order they are supposed to go in.

- Remember the questions you want to ask during conversations as they are happening.

- Make sense of events and occurrences that happen over time.

Activities that will improve your working memory can be:

- Use your math skills. Calculate discounts, tips, and totals while shopping. Do this in your mind to strengthen your working memory.

- Sit in a group or at a party and play a storytelling game. One person starts the story, the next person repeats what is said and adds a little more to the story, and the story continues until everyone has repeated and added to the story.

- Listen to audiobooks. Whereas inhibitory practices will develop in a specific way with audiobooks, when you use them, you are also improving your working memory by ingesting and absorbing details where you can relate to new information.

- Perform poetry or slam poetry out loud. This will have you memorizing short bursts of words and build your attention. As a side note, you do not have to perform the poetry in front of anyone, just say the poems aloud and build on your memory skills (Diamond, 2022).

Cognitive flexibility includes the ability to:

- Think outside the box.

- See other people's perspectives.

- Take a chance on a sudden opportunity.

- Find success despite challenges or barriers.

- Adjust to unexpected issues that occur.

- Admit you were wrong after you hear new information.

If you are looking for activities to improve your cognitive flexibility, try some of the ideas below:

- Improvise. Participate in theater programs and music lessons that encourage creativity with a need to adjust quickly. Some examples can be jazz and dance.

- Use out-of-the-box objects. Come up with unique uses for everyday objects. For example, use your kitchen table for something else other than eating. Could it be a fort? A drum? What else? Pens can be used to write, but they can also hold hair up in a bun, clean out tight spots, and other things.

- Look for common items. Find common traits between daily items. How are carrots and cucumbers similar? How is your car like a foot? Come up with a list of daily items and find out how they can connect.

- Solve real-life problems. As typical as this exercise sounds, solving everyday problems is part of your daily routine, even if it is not in your job description. When you come across a problem, do you try to troubleshoot until you resolve it, or do you pass it off to someone else because you "cannot" do something? Instead of pulling the trigger and handing the problem to someone else, try to solve the problem yourself unless you find that someone will get hurt because of it.

If none of the items above sound interesting, you can find other places to improve your executive function skills in the activities below:

- Learn how to cook and bake.

- Find creative outlets like crafting or painting.

- Caring for animals, children, the elderly, etc.

- Engage in the arts like theater, dance, or music

- Join a league or sports team.

- Participate in martial arts.

- Learn how to survive in the wild.

- Practice woodworking.

The activities above involve planning, perseverance, creative problem-solving, and cognitive flexibility, which marries all the executive function skills together.

Executive functions are also a precursor to stress and self-esteem. When your stress levels are high and your self-esteem is low, your executive function skills may seem as though they are on the fritz. Below are some methods to help lower your stress levels and build your self-image. Try them out and see what works best for you.

- **Ask for help**. You cannot do everything on your own, despite what society says you have to or should do. It is wrong to assume that you must "do it all." Instead, find strength by reaching out for help and getting advice, guidance, and information you would not have known otherwise. It may bruise your ego, but once you are in a good role with it, you will see how incredible it can seem.

- **Build a stable routine**. Find predictability, clarity, and consistency with what you will and will not accept in your daily life. This process can take a little work but will help you reduce stress and build confidence by creating healthy boundaries at work, at home, and with friends.

- **Understand that mistakes are part of the learning process**. Making a mistake is not a bad thing. It is an opportunity to stretch your current abilities and to help you learn something new. Having a growth mindset will build your confidence and give you a chance to rewrite the directive you have on how to treat yourself when errors occur.

- **Get a pet**. Even though a huge responsibility comes with owning a pet, these fuzzy little guys will help improve your mood and reduce stress (Barker et al., 38; Gee et al., 230; R. T. Barker et al. 29).

- Find self-compassion. When you learn how to be kind to yourself despite the mistakes you make and the flaws you have, you begin to teach yourself that being perfect is not the goal to strive for. Also, compassion for yourself leads to compassion for others, so you are helping out more people than you realize.

- **Exercise**. Getting into a moving action will relieve much stress. Also, activities where you burn energy, encourage healthy sleep habits, release more chemicals in your brain, and will keep you in a healthier state of mind.

- **Be mindful**. When you move and think with mindful intentions, you are allowing yourself to build up every part of executive functionality and granting yourself a reprieve from your ADHD symptoms. Daily mindfulness will make you aware of your actions and thoughts before they happen and will give you the chance to forgive yourself when you respond in a different way than you wanted to (Diamond, 2022).

Exercise Ten: Self-Reflection of Executive Function Skills

Now that you have read up on executive function skills and know where it connects with you, you can think about different times in your day when executive dysfunction may slide into place over the functionality. Make a list below in each section to see your issues with time management, organization, planning, problem-solving, self-awareness, and more.

Once you discover where your pain points are, you can develop goals and create a plan to move forward on strengthening your skills.

Where do I have issues with Time Management?

For example, I am rarely on time

_____

_____

_____

_____

_____

_____

_____

_____

_____

_____

_____

_____

_____

_____

_____

_____

Where do I have planning issues?

For example, I can never plan to go to the grocery store, even though I mean to do it.

_____

_____

_____

_____

_____

_____

_____

_____

_____

_____

_____

_____

_____

What do I have trouble remembering?

For example, I usually forget about my children's performances, events, and meetings until the day I have to scramble around to make everything work.

_____
_____
_____
_____
_____
_____
_____
_____
_____
_____
_____
_____
_____
_____
_____
_____
_____
_____

How quickly do I get angry?

_____
_____
_____
_____
_____
_____
_____
_____
_____
_____
_____
_____

How often do I get absorbed in a project because it is so interesting? What kind of activities, events, and people do I forget because of it?

For example, I recently discovered Jam Making. I became obsessed, bought all the tools and supplies needed, forgot to pick up my daughter from school one day, and let the laundry pile up to the point that I was overwhelmed and did not want to do it.

_____

_____

_____

_____

_____

_____

_____

_____

_____

_____

How often do I get interested in a subject and become so hyperfocused initially, and when the thrill dies away, I leave the project where it is and never finish it?

For instance, I really enjoy knitting. I knit so much that I decide I want to sell my wares. Halfway through setting up an Etsy store, it becomes too frustrating, I get too tired, and then I have never gotten around to selling them.

_____

_____

_____

_____

_____

_____

_____

_____

_____

You can create more lists and categories based on other information in this chapter. When you write things down, you'll have an amazing opportunity to see the thoughts in your head and build a better form of self-reflection.

Once you have the list created above and can see where your main trigger points are, you can begin to build goals for where you want to be and how you want to strengthen your executive function skill set. See the next exercise and map out some of your goals.

Exercise Eleven: Goals for Building Executive Function Skills

You can build your executive function skills by planning out how to build executive function skills. You are probably right if that sentence seems redundant, but the sentiment is not. Like in the previous section, where you read about solving daily, real-life problems, this exercise allows you to do just that by mapping out goals, breaking them into chunks, setting deadlines, and building skills that can improve your life's structure. See the example below and follow the breadcrumbs to build a goal and deadline that works for you.

Example goal map:

Goal: I want to remember people's names more often.

Deadline: Three months.

Step (Chunk) One: When I meet a new person, repeat their name. For example, "Hello, Shirley, it is nice to meet you." And "I hope you have a nice day, Shirley." When they walk away, repeat their name to yourself one last time.

Deadline: One month. Meet new people by asking individuals for help. You can ask sales representatives for their names at stores, gas stations, etc.

Step (Chunk) Two: When you see them again, ask them what their name is. You can politely say, "Excuse me, can you tell me your name again?" That way, you can remind yourself if you are right, wrong, or forgotten.

Deadline: The next time you see this person.

Step (Chunk) Three: Call them by their name each time you see them.

<u>Deadline</u>: any time after your second encounter. Do not be afraid to ask them for their name again if you forget.

<u>Notes</u>: Once you get into the habit of remembering people's names, you will not be able to say that you are no longer good with names. Instead, you will find that you remember most people's names more often than not.

Your Turn: Try three goals to build executive function skills

<u>Goal One</u>:

_____

_____

_____

<u>Deadline</u>:

_____

_____

<u>Step (Chunk) One</u>:

_____

_____

_____

<u>Deadline</u>:

_____

_____

_____

<u>Step (Chunk) Two</u>:

_____

_____

_____

Deadline:

_____

_____

_____

Step (Chunk) Three:

_____

_____

_____

Deadline:

_____

_____

_____

Notes:

_____

_____

_____

_____

_____

_____

_____

_____

_____

_____

_____

_____

_____

_____

_____

_____

_____

_____

_____

_____

_____

_____

Goal Two:

_____

_____

_____

Deadline:

_____

_____

_____

Step (Chunk) One:

_____

_____

_____

Deadline:

_____

_____

_____

Step (Chunk) Two:

_____

_____

_____

Deadline:

_____

_____

_____

Step (Chunk) Three:

_____

_____

_____

Deadline:

_____

_____

_____

Notes:

_____

_____

_____

_____

_____

Goal Three:

_____

_____

_____

Deadline:

_____

_____

_____

Step (Chunk) One:

_____

_____

_____

_____

Deadline:

_____

_____

_____

_____

Step (Chunk) Two:

_____

_____

_____

_____

Deadline:

_____

_____

_____

_____

Step (Chunk) Three:

_____

_____

_____

_____

Deadline:

_____
_____
_____

Notes:

_____
_____
_____
_____
_____
_____
_____
_____
_____
_____
_____
_____
_____
_____
_____
_____

Once you build your three goals, incorporate one of them into your schedule or routine at a time to avoid getting overwhelmed by new practices. When you find that your interest is waning, make sure to keep going with the project. This part is where you must develop some determination and commitment with self-awareness.

Completing goals will help build confidence in yourself and give you the resolution with executive function.

Conclusion

With the development of any latent executive function skills, you will build self-confidence and feel you can manage life a little better. You will have a plan where you can implement new goals and create new milestones to climb. The more you do this practice, the more it will infuse into your daily life until the method becomes automatic whenever you have a goal or plan you want to tackle.

In the next chapter, you will learn about emotional regulation and rejection sensitivity.

CHAPTER FOUR

Emotional Regulation & Rejection Sensitivity

Introduction

There are times when our emotions get out of hand. There are other times when we are perfectly fine. And yet there are a few times when our emotions feel like they will blow a circuit.

In this seemingly never-ending cycle of emotional ups and downs, it cannot be easy to find kindness for yourself, especially if you have been labeled with one of those tags that assertive, emotive, and expressive women some (most) times receive. The "overly emotional," "crybaby," "insane," etc. are names that do not reflect who you are as a person but follow you around like a black cloud nonetheless.

First, you should know that emotional dysregulation is a huge symptom for women dealing with ADHD. Emotional dysregulation is caused by a lack of chemicals released in your brain to make it function like a neurotypical brain. When this happens, it becomes harder to control where, when, why, and how your emotions implode.

While this is not your fault, you can work on managing it to the point where it will barely seem like a blip on your radar.

This chapter will discuss emotional regulation and rejection sensitivity.

These two topics go hand in hand. The more rejection you felt as a child, the less you can regulate your emotions. The rejection you had when you were a child may have been real, or it may have been a perception of your insecurity. Rejection Sensitivity Dysphoria (RSD) connects with your womanhood, ADHD, and feelings in a way that may blow up your day when you feel attached.

In the book Women with ADHD, we shared a sentiment with our readers. This sentiment still holds today. Please see it below.

"If you have issues with emotional regulation, we hope that by reading this information, you will find relief and know that you are affected not because of your personality but by how your brain developed. Understand that RSD can be managed by introducing healthy coping mechanisms into your daily life (Davis & Hill, 2022)."

What is Emotional Regulation?

Anyone with ADHD can have issues with regulating their emotions. If you feel as though your feelings are on a rollercoaster and you are unsure of what will happen at any given time, you can become confused, bewildered, and befuddled by your emotions and how they react when something doesn't happen the way you anticipate it should.

Emotional regulation is the opposite of dysregulation.

When you are emotionally deregulated, you have an impaired ability to control emotional responses when in certain situations. This dysregulation leads to overblown and extreme reactions that will not fit the circumstances. Some of the symptoms are:

- Reactions that seem out of sync with what happened.

- You cannot calm down, even when aware of your overreaction.

- Become frustrated or annoyed easily—have a low tolerance for this.

- Getting overwhelmed by your emotions.

- Prone to sudden outbursts or are increasingly temperamental.

- Having a difficult time calming down.

When your emotions are deregulated, you will feel like you go from zero to 100 in the blink of an eye. Triggers can be all around you and seemingly random, and you can get frustrated because your preferred yogurt is sold out at the grocery store or you did not get the promotion at work. Do not let your disappointment grow overwhelming.

The key is to separate your emotions from reality. Eventually, you can ask yourself: How important is this? What is a rational response to the disappointing situation?

However, first, you must recognize your emotional dysregulation and see how it affects every element of your life.

Emotional dysregulation can be the most disruptive part of ADHD.

The inability to moderate your response in any environment, like work, home, or socially, can change how people, co-workers, friends, and family members view and interact with you. If you have a temperamental or hypersensitive label at work, you may suffer for it, promotion-wise. You may also put too much undue stress on yourself and focus on the small details instead of looking at the bigger picture.

With personal and romantic relationships, minor issues can become a full blow until your partner, friends, and family may distance themselves from you because they no longer wish to walk on eggshells.

This emotional imbalance can also lead to low self-esteem, self-doubt, and uncertainty about what to do when something arises. Reacting as though every hurdle is catastrophic can become physically and mentally exhausting. There may be times when you just feel as though you want to give up (Green and Colemen, 2022).

Emotional dysregulation is a common symptom of ADHD, although it is rarely discussed. Science has shown that there are too many causes of emotional dysregulation with ADHD. These include an overactive amygdala and an underactive frontal cortex (Shaw et al., 2014).

Your amygdala triggers emotional responses, so when one is overactive, your emotional responses to smaller issues may be much bigger than they need to be. Then, your frontal cortex inhibits and filters emotions so you can react accordingly.

However, when your frontal cortex underreacts, you will have latent responses to controlling your emotions. Combining these two factors will lead to impulsivity, hypersensitivity, and explosions.

You will find five dimensions of a neurotypical brain and how they work with emotional regulation. These levels are listed below:

1. Recognize your emotions

2. Recognize emotions in others.

3. Emotional Reactivity—what is your threshold, how intense are your emotions, and how long do these emotions last?

4. How to reduce your aroused emotions.

5. How to improve your mood and generate better emotions (Green and Colemen, 2022).

Women with ADHD struggle the most with number three. Suppose you consider that your amygdala is overreacting and generates tense feelings that can push the emotional threshold to the limit more often and quickly.

Exercise Twelve: How Are My Emotions Dysregulated?

For this exercise, you will need to become more aware of your emotions and how you react. Even if you think you were justified with your reaction, you need to address the situation from a more objective standpoint and look at different perspectives.

Instructions:

- Write down an instance where you emotionally blew up.

- Examine your reaction. Ask yourself:

  o What happened?

  o What triggered your reaction?

- ○ How did it feel when you were reacting?

- ○ Could you have reacted differently?

- How did the other person respond?

- When you answer these questions, be honest and objective. Do this three times for exercise twelve, but continue to look at your emotional reactions and reflect on how they could be approached differently and if the situation really needed such a big reaction.

- **Emotional Reaction One:**

_____
_____
_____

What happened?

_____
_____
_____

What triggered your reaction?

_____
_____
_____

How did it feel when you were reacting?

_____
_____
_____
_____

Could you have reacted differently?

_____

_____

_____

How did the other person respond?

_____

_____

_____

- **Emotional Reaction Two:**

_____

_____

_____

What happened?

_____

_____

_____

What triggered your reaction?

_____

_____

_____

How did it feel when you were reacting?

_____

_____

_____

_____

Could you have reacted differently?

_____

_____

_____

How did the other person respond?

_____

_____

_____

- **Emotional Reaction Three:**

_____

_____

_____

What happened?

_____

_____

_____

What triggered your reaction?

_____

_____

_____

How did it feel when you were reacting?

_____

_____

_____

_____

Could you have reacted differently?

_____

_____

_____

How did the other person respond?

_____

_____

_____

Once you have filled out three instances, do not stop with your self-reflection. Instead, use this exercise to spur new examinations each time you react in a way that seems over the top. While you can use self-reflection and self-awareness tools to observe your reactions, try some of the strategies below. These methods can help you build a better routine when your emotions rise.

- **Name your emotions**. If you are feeling angry, frustrated, happy, giddy, etc., and it seems overblown, name the emotion you are feeling. Then, redirect yourself differently before you react. You can try some of the following ideas to see if they help distract you from the big emotion:

  o Leave. Move from whatever room you are in and leave the situation. Stand in the backyard, get a drink of water, go for a walk, or more. If you have another person involved, tell them you need to take a few minutes so you can catch your breath and process your feelings.

  o Be aware of what your body is doing. Are you sweating? Do you find it hard to breathe? Can you feel your heart race?

  o Describe the feeling you have named. Be as specific as possible. You can write about this, talk it out with another person, or just say the information out loud and to an empty room.

- **Make an emotional journal**. Getting your emotions out onto the paper gets them out of your head and heart. If you can pour them out of yourself without physical, mental, and emotional harm to anyone, you may feel some relief. This process is an active way of expressing yourself, even if no one else hears it.

- **Exercise**. Women with ADHD struggle to disengage their emotions from their thoughts and actions. If you find that you cannot calm down, go work out. Exerting physical energy can use up excessive stress and burn off that overblown feeling. This energy depletion can help you avoid yelling and screaming and can help you sort through the real problem.

- **Use music**. You can play an instrument or listen to music. When you do this, your mood will improve.

- **Make a list of coping mechanisms**. Like journaling your emotions, getting a list of coping mechanisms in front of you can get the ideas out of your head and give you a sense of accomplishment. Developing a list of coping tools will be proactive instead of reactive, which is training your brain and body to behave when other items come to pass (Green and Colemen, 2022).

- **Try ADHD medication**. While this method can be controversial, when you use medication, you are helping your brain work by filling it up with the chemicals and hormones it needs. Medicine (especially in the present) will not change who you are, what you do, how you feel, what you say, or how you think. It can help you an incredible amount, and you will be able to breathe easier. However, if you are not comfortable taking medication for any reason, you do not have to do it. Follow your gut here. You may be scared to take meds, but know it is the right choice, or you may understand that you are not ready to take that step. Either one is okay.

- **Be mindful.** Hey! Here is the buzzword "mindful" again. This time it is about emotional regulation. Mindfulness works on many levels. Incorporating mindfulness meditation into your daily life will encourage self-awareness and build a desire for growth (Bertin, 2022).

When you understand how your emotions work and how you can help regulate them, you will also see and feel your sensitivity to rejection dwindle.

What is Rejection Sensitivity?

Rejection sensitivity dysphoria (RSD) manifests emotional regulation and seriously disrupts a woman's life. If you have ADHD and have not been diagnosed until adulthood, you may have formed these symptoms over the years due to fear of rejection. Dysphoria comes into play because although you were not traumatized by rejection, you begin to see, feel, and hear rejection even with the most constructive critiques.

Women with ADHD have often described RSD as an open wound. And when they face rejection (real or dysmorphic), they will be overcome by intense pain that sometimes exposes them to extreme emotional reactions. If you have RSD with your ADHD, you have developed this disorder because you have never found healthy or effective ways to cope with your symptoms or the pain of rejection (Davis & Hill, 2022).

Rejection can be an enormous trigger point for you. Your sensitivity to rejection, whether real or perceived, can make different interactions a source of pain. Even when you feel there is a possibility of rejection, you can begin to avoid many things. When you avoid potential rejection, you can stop yourself from trying new things, taking chances in your career, and even being fearful of breaking away from chaos (Dodson & Saline, 2022).

Our book Women with ADHD rejects sensitivity at length and how it can even elicit shame and cause a more open willingness to engage in sexual activities because sex equals social acceptance.

"You [may] have already taken part in risky sexual behavior or have thought about it often. You may have also had younger initiations into intercourse and other sexual activity, more casual sex, more sexual partners, and less protected sex with more transmissible sexual infections. You may have even had more unplanned pregnancies because of unsafe sexual practices (Davis & Hill, 2022; Dodson & Saline, 2022)."

Of course, rejection sensitivity is more than just having too many sexual encounters or fear of trying new things. Dr. William Dodson LF-APA writes for *ADDitude* online frequently. In his article, "How ADHD Ignites Rejection Sensitive Dysphoria (2022),"

Dodson writes:

"Rejection sensitive dysphoria is one manifestation of emotional dysregulation, a common but misunderstood and under-researched symptom of ADHD in adults. Individuals with RSD feel 'unbearable' pain as a result of perceived or actual rejection, teasing, or criticism that is not alleviated with cognitive or dialectical behavior therapy."

What Dodson is explaining is the pain and anxiety that comes from even an idea of rejection—this happens when someone experiences brain-based symptoms that are traumatic but not caused by trauma when it comes to rejection. While it is not a formal diagnosis of ADHD, it is pegged as a "disruptive manifestation of emotional dysregulation—a common, but under-researched and misunderstood symptom of ADHD, particularly in adults (2022)."

One-third of adult patients with ADHD report that they have RSD and that it is the most paralyzing part of their disorder because they cannot find ways to cope or manage the pain RSD can cause.

Rejection Sensitive Dysphoria can be caused by rejection, teasing, criticism, and negative self–talk prompted by contrived or real failures. It is characterized by "intense mood shifts triggered by distinct episodes following the previous causes (Dodson, 2022).

Review some of the outward signs of RSD to see if any of them sound familiar:

- Emotional outbursts that follow criticism or rejection, whether real or contrived.

- Avoidance of social situations.

- Thoughts of self-harm or negative self-talk.

- Poor perception of self or low self-esteem.

- Negative and continuous self-talk can be seen as "being your own worst enemy."

- Recurring and ruminating thoughts.

- Problems with relationships, constantly feeling rejected or defensive.

Although there is always a slight change in misdiagnosis, understanding the difference between a mood disorder, like social anxiety, and RSD with ADHD can help determine if you should pursue other options.

If you have a mood disorder, your symptoms will look more like the following:

- Untriggered mood changes (often seemingly out of the blue).

- Moods are not reflective of what is going on in our life.

- There is a gradual shift in your mood over the weeks.

- The offset of your mood will last weeks to months.

- The duration of mood shift is two weeks or longer (Dodson, 2022).

For RSD with ADHD, your symptoms will look more like this:

- A clear trigger will shift your mood.

- Your mood will match your perception of the trigger.

- Your mood shift will be instant.

- Your mood will shift back to "normal" within hours.

While RSD is not currently paired with ADHD in the DSM–5–TR—meaning it is not a formal symptom of ADHD in the United States—in the European Union, it is one of the six fundamental features of an ADHD diagnosis. And while there is a big push to include RSD in an official ADHD diagnosis, there may be reasons why it may never happen:

- RSD episodes are not always present.

- It comes in triggered bursts and is hard to measure.

- Those with RSD are usually ashamed of their over-reactions and hide them to avoid being labeled mentally unstable or overly emotional (Dodson, 2022).

Rejection sensitivity dysphoria is a serious issue that can be managed and even turned around with help through talk therapy and a behavioral treatment plan. Dodson claims that "[RSD] is difficult for people with ADHD to describe, but all who have it agree that it feels awful. Indeed, the term dysphoria is literally Greek for 'unbearable (2002).'"

You may not have RSD, you may secretly see some of the symptoms in your actions, or you may suspect that you have this part of ADHD. Take the quiz below to give yourself a better idea about it. The quiz is not meant to diagnose you with RSD. This quiz is manifested in Dr. William Dodson's work and is meant for personal use that will help you discover whether a clinical evaluation is needed.

Exercise Thirteen: Do You Have Rejection Sensitivity?

Instructions: Check the box that resonates most with your actions, thoughts, behaviors, and emotions.

When your feelings are hurt, do you experience intense bouts of rage?

- Very Often
- Rarely

- Often
- Never

- Sometimes

When you feel that you have been criticized or rejected, do you experience extreme bouts of sadness?

- Very Often
- Rarely

- Often
- Never

- Sometimes

Do you judge yourself harder than you judge others?

- Very Often
- Often

- Sometimes
- Never
- Rarely

Do you assume no one likes you, so you avoid social situations, or assume you will have anxiety no matter what?

- Very Often
- Rarely
- Often
- Never
- Sometimes

Do you see yourself going above and beyond to get on someone's good side? Do you consider yourself a people pleaser?

- Very Often
- Rarely
- Often
- Never
- Sometimes

Do you pass on opportunities at work or home because you are afraid you will fail (or not complete them)?

- Very Often
- Rarely
- Often
- Never
- Sometimes

Has anyone called you "overly sensitive," "overly emotional," "a head case," etc., due to your strong emotional reactions?

- Very Often
- Rarely
- Often
- Never
- Sometimes

Do you often feel pressured to be "perfect" to avoid making mistakes and thereby getting rejected or a bad critique?

- Very Often
- Often
- Sometimes
- Rarely
- Never

Do you experience physical emotions, like you have been punched in the chest or physically "wounded?"

- Very Often
- Often
- Sometimes
- Rarely
- Never

Are you often ashamed of how you cannot seem to control your emotions?

- Very Often
- Often
- Sometimes
- Rarely
- Never

Have you been told you had a mood or borderline character disorder before you were diagnosed with ADHD?

- Very Often
- Often
- Sometimes
- Rarely
- Never

Is it easier to evade intimate relationships with friends or romantically? Are you worried that they will not like the "real you" if they get too close?

- Very Often
- Often

- Sometimes
- Never
- Rarely

Do you constantly fear that you will be fired every time your boss calls you into their office? Do you assume that commonplace interactions will always end up terribly?

- Very Often
- Rarely
- Often
- Never
- Sometimes

Do you believe that you cannot continue feeling the way you do?

- Very Often
- Rarely
- Often
- Never
- Sometimes

Do you avoid going to new places, trying new things, or meeting new people, because you fear failure, rejection, or criticism?

- Very Often
- Often
- Sometimes

- Rarely
- Never

(Dodson, 2022)

Once you fill out the questionnaire above, take some time to reflect on it. If you have answered sometimes, often, or very often more questions than not, that could be an indicator of RSD. However, you will not know for sure until you get a formal diagnosis from a clinical evaluation.

Suppose you have received a clinical evaluation and formal diagnosis. In this case, you may find that you and your mental health provider have developed a plan to divert RSD into something healthier for you to manage.

If you and your medical health professional have begun developing a behavioral treatment plan, which may or may not include medicine, you may develop mindfulness activities. Mindfulness activities will allow you to be in the moment of your emotions and thoughts, but instead of connecting to them, you will observe them from an objective position.

You can start with the exercise below that will help you start to reframe the ruminating self-deprecating thoughts and have you redirect your negative, intense emotions into a more positive way.

The exercise below will help you reframe negative thoughts and redirect uncomfortable emotions into a more positive overview.

Exercise Fourteen: How to Redirect RSD to Positivity

This activity will have you taking an objective stance on many of your more unpleasant emotions, thoughts, and feelings regarding RSD. You can begin by thinking about five to eight examples of when your RSD got the better of you. Then, you can map out the trigger, your emotions, your actions, and your calming moment. Afterward, you can reflect on how you could have handled the situation differently.

RSD is part of how your brain behaves. It may take some time to see a shift in your behavior, but with practice and persistence, you will be able to catch yourself before you have an RST reaction. You may even get to the point where you see a potential trigger and extinguish it before you get an opportunity to feel rejected without having to avoid circumstances, people, or experiences.

Instructions:

1. Think of a time when your RSD was triggered.

2. Explain what happened without giving in to the extreme emotions connected to the memory and without judging yourself, your actions, or your emotions.

3. Map out the trigger point, your actions, and how you felt about it.

4. Do you see moments where you could have done things differently?

This practice is one of mindfulness. Any insight into your behavior can prepare you for the next time things happen.

Memory One:

What happened?

_____

_____

_____

What was the trigger?

_____

_____

_____

What did you feel?

_____

_____

_____

What were your actions?

_____

_____

_____

What could you have done differently?

_____

_____

_____

Memory Two:

What happened?

_____

_____

_____

What was the trigger?

_____

_____

_____

What did you feel?

_____

_____

_____

What were your actions?

_____

_____

_____

What could you have done differently?

_____

_____

_____

Memory Three:

What happened?

_____

_____

_____

What was the trigger?

_____

_____

_____

What did you feel?

_____

_____

_____

What were your actions?

_____

_____

_____

What could you have done differently?

_____

_____

_____

Memory Four:

What happened?

_____

_____

_____

What was the trigger?

_____

_____

_____

What did you feel?

_____

_____

_____

What were your actions?

_____

_____

_____

_____

What could you have done differently?

_____

_____

_____

Memory Five:

What happened?

_____

_____

_____

What was the trigger?

_____

_____

_____

What did you feel?

_____

_____

_____

What were your actions?

_____

_____

_____

_____

What could you have done differently?

_____

_____

_____

_____

Memory Six:

What happened?

_____

_____

_____

What was the trigger?

_____

_____

_____

What did you feel?

_____

_____

_____

What were your actions?

_____

_____

_____

_____

What could you have done differently?

_____

_____

_____

_____

Memory Seven:

What happened?

_____

_____

_____

What was the trigger?

_____

_____

_____

What did you feel?

_____

_____

_____

What were your actions?

_____

_____

_____

_____

What could you have done differently?

_____

_____

_____

_____

Memory Eight:

What happened?

_____

_____

_____

What was the trigger?

_____

_____

_____

What did you feel?

_____

_____

_____

What were your actions?

_____

_____

_____

_____

What could you have done differently?

_____

_____

_____

_____

Just because you feel rejection does not mean that rejection is the intent of the other person. Your RSD will give you an overinflated sense of negative criticism when it is more about how your brain behaves.

Exercise Fifteen: RSD Mirror—Finding Out Where You're Sensitive

Once you begin pinning the negative self-talk in your mind and you can recognize what you are saying to yourself, you can find out just where your triggers are. Use the trigger points above to see where things are sensitive. Ask yourself the following questions:

- What is the trigger?

- Why is this a trigger for me?

- Do I remember the moment or feeling of the trigger?

- Where have I been triggered like this in the past?

Use this exercise to mirror yourself and pull out some introspective thoughts. You may have a difficult time touching these emotions, and they may feel rawer than what you are expecting, so it is always important, if you have a negative reaction at first, to talk with your therapist about these things. If you feel more comfortable working through this exercise with your therapist, at least at the beginning, that is also perfectly acceptable. That idea will be applauded.

Memory One

_____

_____

_____

What is the trigger?

_____

_____

_____

Why is this a trigger for me?

_____

_____

_____

Do I remember the moment or feeling of the trigger?

_____

_____

_____

Where have I been triggered like this in the past?

_____

_____

_____

Memory Two

_____

_____

_____

What is the trigger?

_____

_____

_____

Why is this a trigger for me?

_____

_____

_____

Do I remember the moment or feeling of the trigger?

_____

_____

_____

Where have I been triggered like this in the past?

_____

_____

_____

Memory Three

_____

_____

_____

What is the trigger?

_____

_____

_____

Why is this a trigger for me?

_____

_____

_____

Do I remember the moment or feeling of the trigger?

_____

_____

_____

Where have I been triggered like this in the past?

_____

_____

_____

Memory Four

_____

_____

_____

What is the trigger?

_____

_____

_____

Why is this a trigger for me?

_____

_____

_____

Do I remember the moment or feeling of the trigger?

_____

_____

_____

Where have I been triggered like this in the past?

_____

_____

_____

Memory Five

_____

_____

_____

What is the trigger?

_____

_____

_____

Why is this a trigger for me?

_____

_____

_____

Do I remember the moment or feeling of the trigger?

_____

_____

_____

Where have I been triggered like this in the past?

_____

_____

_____

Memory Six

_____

_____

_____

What is the trigger?

_____

_____

_____

Why is this a trigger for me?

_____

_____

_____

Do I remember the moment or feeling of the trigger?

_____

_____

_____

Where have I been triggered like this in the past?

_____

_____

_____

Memory Seven

_____

_____

_____

What is the trigger?

_____

_____

_____

Why is this a trigger for me?

_____

_____

_____

_____

Do I remember the moment or feeling of the trigger?

_____

_____

_____

Where have I been triggered like this in the past?

_____

_____

_____

Memory Eight

_____

_____

_____

What is the trigger?

_____

_____

_____

Why is this a trigger for me?

_____

_____

_____

Do I remember the moment or feeling of the trigger?

_____

_____

_____

Where have I been triggered like this in the past?

_____

_____

_____

Acceptance—Break The Silence And Take Center Stage

By the time you are an adult, you have learned to hide your ADHD symptoms, especially if you have had to conform to certain ideas of what a woman, wife, mom, etc., should be like. You may just be trying to fit in and be "normal." Alternatively, you may have rejected the entire idea of societal norms and are living a different kind of life.

No matter your approach to your ADHD-ness, you will still have to accept that part of yourself. Just as you have learned to accept, your hormones will be in flux, and anytime you get on a phone call, your child will need you as if it is the most important thing in the entire world (if you are a mother).

Problems occur if you do not begin to accept the issues that ADHD can bring into your life. Two of the most common occurrences are low self-esteem and self-harm. Most women struggle with their internalized sense of impairments, which affects their sense of self and how they manage their life skills.

Many women even believe they are not entitled to a support system because they are where everyone else comes to get support, which could not be further from the truth.

You may also blame yourself for being too distracted to catch up on daily responsibilities. You may allow your disorganization, lateness, and lack of motivation to be an excuse for people to reject or criticize you. You may begin censoring yourself.

When your premenstrual hormone levels fluctuate, you can experience various ADHD symptoms, such as higher rates of irritability, negative moods, sleep issues, and trouble focusing. These symptoms can easily lead to chronic stress and a possible misdiagnosis of PMDD.

Developing a plan to accept your ADHD symptoms and the idea of ADHD has an easy fix for finding confidence in your actions. And while that is easier than it sounds, the first step you can take is figuring out where you doubt yourself the most and where your lowest self-esteem points are.

Exercise Sixteen: Self-Reflection, Where Do You Doubt Yourself the Most?

We all have insecurities. They can nag us or tell us we are wrong, and when someone tells you something nice about yourself, insecurity can cause you not to believe them (more on that below). However, not everyone is insecure and allows those negative self-doubting words to bother them. If you find that you get anchored down into negative self-talk and let your brain walk all over your insecurity, this exercise is for you.

This is a self-reflection exercise where you will write down the negative thoughts and feelings about yourself, examine those, where they came from, why they are there, and work on shifting those into a new, more positive direction.

This exercise is not built to make you feel bad about yourself nor should you indulge the thoughts and emotions that come across when attempting this exercise. This is an objective study of why you feel what you feel when you feel it. If you find that the negative thoughts about yourself start to stick or make you feel low, you can swat them away like the bugs that they are. This exercise isn't meant to feed them, instead it's going to help you beat them.

Negative Thought One

_____
_____
_____
_____

Why do I think this way?

_____
_____
_____
_____

Where did it come from?

_____

_____

_____

How can I rewrite the thought/feeling?

_____

_____

_____

Negative Thought Two

_____

_____

_____

Why do I think this way?

_____

_____

_____

Where did it come from?

_____

_____

_____

How can I rewrite the thought/feeling?

_____

_____

_____

Negative Thought Three

_____

_____

_____

Why do I think this way?

_____

_____

_____

Where did it come from?

_____

_____

_____

How can I rewrite the thought/feeling?

_____

_____

_____

Negative Thought Four

_____

_____

_____

Why do I think this way?

_____

_____

_____

_____

Where did it come from?

_____

_____

_____

How can I rewrite the thought/feeling?

_____

_____

_____

Negative Thought Five

_____

_____

_____

Why do I think this way?

_____

_____

_____

Where did it come from?

_____

_____

_____

How can I rewrite the thought/feeling?

_____

_____

_____

If you feel as though your emotions become unstable, it is always okay to stop the exercise above and take it slow. You will not have to do the memories all at once, nor will you have to do them alone. This exercise is something you can do with a therapist or counselor present.

Exercise Seventeen: Nice things People Say to Me—Here is Why I reject them.

There are a lot of things you might not be able to accept when someone says something nice. Whether it is about your appearance, kindness, work, or whatever, your first instinct may be to reject what someone says by waving it off, blushing, or saying, "No, I'm not." That's how many of us react, but that doesn't mean we should. Compliments and things others say about you are meant to make you feel good, so why don't you let yourself? What are you afraid will happen if you say, "Thank you, I appreciate the kind words." Nothing bad can come from it, and you are probably due to having someone say something nice because they mean it and because it is true.

There is an ongoing debate about how many good things we need to hear about erasing the bad things we tell ourselves. Some say the ratio is five nice things to every negative thing; others say three, and some say seven. Regardless of the number, the point is still the same: we do not treat ourselves very well.

But you will have to take that step to boost self-esteem and crush self-doubt. While this isn't always easy, it is good to learn to accept, take, and give genuine compliments. Although you must figure out why you reject them, you must first realize how you react to compliments.

This exercise is built to help you recognize your reaction to compliments. Like the previous exercises, you can recall memories of someone saying something nice. But then, remember what you said back. Was your first reaction a quick "No?" Did you wave your hand off and say, "You do not have to say that?" Or did you become embarrassed?

Each reaction is normal, especially when you don't want to hear something nice about yourself. You deserve to hear something nice about how you are. You are smart, strong, kind, funny, and so much more. However, if you have self-esteem issues, it will be much harder to take the compliment and sit with it than block the kindness coming your way.

Nice thing someone said to me:

_____

_____

_____

My Reaction—what I said:

_____

_____

_____

How I felt:

_____

_____

_____

Nice thing someone said to me:

_____

_____

_____

My Reaction—what I said:

_____

_____

_____

How I felt:

_____

_____

_____

Nice thing someone said to me:

_____

_____

_____

My Reaction—what I said:

_____

_____

_____

How I felt:

_____

_____

_____

Nice thing someone said to me:

_____

_____

_____

My Reaction—what I said:

_____

_____

_____

How I felt:

_____

_____

_____

Nice thing someone said to me:

_____

_____

_____

My Reaction—what I said:

_____

_____

_____

How I felt:

_____

_____

_____

Nice thing someone said to me:

_____

_____

_____

My Reaction—what I said:

_____

_____

_____

How I felt:

_____

_____

_____

_____

Nice thing someone said to me:

_____

_____

_____

My Reaction—what I said:

_____

_____

_____

How I felt:

_____

_____

_____

Nice thing someone said to me:

_____

_____

_____

My Reaction—what I said:

_____

_____

_____

How I felt:

_____

_____

_____

Nice thing someone said to me:

_____

_____

_____

My Reaction—what I said:

_____

_____

_____

How I felt:

_____

_____

_____

Boost Your Self-Esteem and Crush Self-Doubt

Once you begin to see and feel your knee-jerk reactions to compliments, you may be able to understand why it is hard for you to accept that you are a nice person, but that only gets you over the threshold of confidence building. You will have to boost your confidence. Below is a list of activities to help you build your self-esteem. It is surprisingly easier than it may seem. It takes a little self-care, a dash of intuition, and some building blocks. You will realize that helping yourself helps others, too (so you are really helping yourself to be selfless).

Dr. Peter Jaska, a journalist and clinical psychologist, discusses this in his article, "How to Regain Your Confidence: Life-Changing Strategies for Adults with ADHD." Jaska says:

When ADHD is managed well, this erosion of self-esteem can be prevented. Any emotional damage can also be repaired and reversed.

Remember: None of us is a prisoner of our past, and it is never too late to change.

A strong program of treatment and ADHD management gives a person a fighting chance to manage their ADHD biology and behaviors reasonably (not perfectly) well. This is critical to ending a cycle of frustration and sense of failure (2022).

The past can weigh so heavily on us that we barely realize we are holding it in. These negative emotions can also affect how we look at the world and treat others. The cycle of frustration and sense of failure Jaska describes may be all too relevant to your life, but you have the power to pick yourself up and dust yourself off.

No one is responsible for your emotions, self-confidence, or determination to accept you. People can support you, but you have to let them. You have to ask for help and hear what they are saying. When you are riddled with self-doubt and low self-esteem, it might not be easy to hear constructive things about you from others. However, it is important that you listen to them while you are building yourself up. You can still learn something even if you do not agree with what your support system is saying.

The statement above is not an excuse for someone to say negative and abusive things to you. Instead, it is an opportunity to take pieces of yourself and heal them.

Jaska also suggests what an effective treatment program can look like. This includes ADHD medication, behavioral therapy, ADHD coaching, and self-care like regular sleep, healthy nutrition, and physical activity (2022).

The article "How to Regain Your Confidence" discusses stopping negative thinking and provides the reader with eleven other tools to help yourself feel better and build your self-esteem in a healthy and strong place.

On negative thinking, Jaska says:

"One of the harmful aspects of low self-esteem is the loss of self-confidence and belief that you can change and grow. This feeling can be overcome, but it takes work and persistence. To get "unstuck," adults with ADHD have to recognize, challenge, and dismiss the negative thinking that comes with and contributes to low self-esteem.

Even when these negative messages feel natural, they must not be accepted as normal or healthy. View these messages as cognitive distortions instead. The battle for stronger self-esteem will be long, but it is a battle that can be won" (2022).

The negative messages we tell ourselves are interpretations of things we have learned from our past. Although they feel natural, they are not. Nor are these thoughts healthy. You can win the battle over your self-esteem, not that you will never have a negative idea of yourself again, but with the right tools, you will be able to deal with them more healthily and productively.

Below are eleven helpful tips to start building your confidence:

1. As you accept and understand the biology of your ADHD, you can focus on changing your behavior. Do not think of the disorder as a negative label—you are not broken—that idea is a destructive stigma that diminishes your self-work and self-esteem.

2. Your ADHD is not a defect of your character or a disease to be cured. ADHD is a neurobiological set of manageable symptoms.

3. You are never too old to learn how to make your ADHD better. "I have tried everything" is not a valid excuse, and it is never true. There is always something else to try.

4. Appreciate your accomplishments by identifying them. If you are not sure what to pick, ask three people who support you for their genuine opinions.

5. Understand your strengths and weaknesses. You can ask friends or loved ones as well. Knowing where you can improve and are strong will help you build a better plan. Appreciate the strengths you have. Work on areas where you are weak by setting healthy and realistic goals.

6. Monitor, challenge and dismiss your negative self-talk. It is an ongoing battle and will be waged for as long as it is. While it will get easier over time, you will need persistent practice and the ability to identify the negativity you say to yourself.

7. Do not compare yourself to others. Do not do it. It is never a good idea and can

easily spiral into a negative cycle. Anyone with low self-esteem will almost always find a way to be inferior.

8. Focus on solutions. When you identify your problem, you ask yourself, "What can I do about it," let the problem go and move forward to find the resolution.

9. Forget about the shoulda,' coulda,' woulda,'s. Anything in the past is best left there. You are working toward your future. Move forward with day-by-day progress in mind.

10. Find people who accept and love you for who you are—ADHD and all. Positive relationships will help you find a healthier frame of mind. Steer clear of isolating yourself from social and emotional places. Especially when you are feeling low.

11. Exercise, eat healthily, and sleep well. Taking care of your body will impact your mood incredibly (Jaksa, 2020).

Exercise Eighteen: Build a Positivity Plan

Below, write down one thing from each of the eleven tips that you can do to help yourself. Think about the SMART plan, and make your goals realistic, healthy, and time-relevant.

Plan for Tip One:

_____

_____

Plan for Tip Two:

_____

_____

Plan for Tip Three:

_____

_____

_____

Plan for Tip Four:

_____

_____

Plan for Tip Five:

_____

_____

Plan for Tip Six:

_____

_____

Plan for Tip Seven:

_____

_____

Plan for Tip Eight:

_____

_____

Plan for Tip Nine:

_____

_____

Plan for Tip Ten:

_____

_____

Plan for Tip Eleven:

_____

_____

Once you start to build your confidence, other things in your life will begin to come together as well.

Managing ADHD and your hormones

Hormones play a huge role in every woman's life. When things get out of whack, they can mess up more than your mood. They can mess up how you sleep, how your body feels, how you think, what you crave to eat, and more. If you are a woman with ADHD, hormonal fluctuations can really touch every part of your world.

Dr. Ellen Lippman, a journalist and licensed clinical psychologist, studied girls and women with ADHD. She discovered that "the brain is a target organ for estrogen, where it impacts cognition, mood, and sleep (2012)."

The role hormones play in ADHD shifts drastically each month. Hormone levels fluctuate with the onset of menstruation. These changes include decreases and increases in estrogen, progesterone, and testosterone (CHADD, 2022).

These hormones also play a vital role in sexuality, emotions, reproduction, well-being, and health of the woman. Since test subjects have mostly been male in the past, hormone changes' effect on women with ADHD has not been studied as fluently as it can be, which is a topic that has been noted. Now, according to CHADD.org:

"A growing number of studies show that sex hormones play a role in regulating communications between brain cells and can negatively affect executive function (Barth et al., 2015). Rather than avoiding monthly fluctuations of hormones, Dr. Haimov-Kochman and Dr. Berger suggest new studies should focus on the subtle fluctuations and combinations of hormones that influence emotions and executive function to understand the role of hormones in ADHD.

The endocrine system comprises multiple glands that produce different kinds of hormones (Young, 2022). It is an interconnected system that is slow acting, with long-lasting impacts" (CHADD, 2022).

Now that a growing study shows the connection between sex hormones, brain cells, and their communication, scientists and researchers have begun to uncover how nuanced the ADHD mind is and how differently the disorder affects women.

What You Can Do About Hormones and ADHD

The thing about hormone levels is that you cannot see them. You do not know what they are, and it is rare to understand just how to manage them. When you couple hormones with ADHD, it can lead to a host of issues.

Several factors can affect hormone regulation. Psychosocial, environmental, and physiological factors, along with monthly hormone changes, not including menopause, perimenopause, and puberty, will impact how your symptoms present themselves (CHADD, 2022).

While studies of estrogen and other chemicals are less than ten years old, there are a few things you can do. As of now, you can get your hormone levels tested with your gynecologist or an endocrinologist. It is also a good idea to track your menstrual cycle and see how your cycle corresponds with your ADHD symptoms (CHADD, 2022).

Dr. Patricia Quinn, director of the National Center for Girls and Women with ADHD, wrote in her book *Understanding Women with ADHD* that:

"The average age of diagnosis for women with ADHD, who weren't diagnosed as children, is 36 to 38 years old. Before that time, girls and women were often misdiagnosed as having a mood disorder or an anxiety disorder. Even if these are secondary conditions, treating them does not get to the root of the problem, which is ADHD."

As such, doctors who do not see the connection between hormone levels and ADHD will not develop a proper treatment plan with you on how you can work within the boundaries of these things, which Quinn is looking to rectify.

In the article, "Women, Hormones, and ADHD," Laura Flynn McCarthy, a freelance writer specializing in children and women's health, writes about four stages of the hormonal life of women and offers ways to manage these symptoms.

As odd as it is to separate women into four parts of their life, understand that these are the times when hormone levels waver. While a woman is more than just pubescent, reproductive, pregnant, and menopausal, for the purposes of this section, that is how it is broken down.

Puberty

Girls start puberty between the ages of nine and eleven and, on average, get their period between eleven and fourteen. This is when hormones are bouncing through your body like a ping-pong ball and may have even been pegged as "raging" hormones when you were a child.

If you were a child diagnosed with ADHD and your parents put you on medication, the extra levels of progesterone and estrogen may have diminished how effective the medication was on ADHD. This erasure of help on medication may have even taken away your belief in medication.

Quinn says, "Studies have shown that estrogen may enhance a woman's response to amphetamine medications, but this effect may be diminished in the presence of progesterone (2002)."

Armed with this information, what do you do?

There are a few solutions.

Talk with your doctor or mental health specialist about different medications, their doses, and how long it takes to get used to each medication. Then you can pick the one that is best for you to try. Develop behavioral strategies, time management skills, and improve organization.

If you notice that your symptoms worsen over time or at certain times of the month, finish projects before these times hit, and maybe even discuss different self-care rituals to put in play the week before hormone levels flux (McCarthy & Novotni, "Women, Hormones, and ADHD," 2022).

Reproductive Years

If you are a woman in her reproductive years, you probably feel your ADHD symptoms a little more. Alternatively, if you just got diagnosed, you may now just be recognizing the inattentive, hyper, restless feeling you have close to or on your period has to do with your ADHD and nothing to do with you as a person.

The average menstrual cycle is about twenty-eight days long. This count includes the first day of your period. During the first two weeks of your cycle, things go smoothly for women because this is when progesterone levels rise. The second two weeks are called the luteal phase. This is the third and fourth week when progesterone begins to fall past the beneficial levels, and estrogen's effects on your brain are reduced. This includes using estrogen stimulant medications (McCarthy & Novotni, "Women, Hormones, and ADHD," 2022).

Quinn believes that PMS is more acute in women who have ADHD. "Feelings of sadness and anxiety typically worsen in women with ADHD during this time (2002)."

Solutions for a woman in her reproductive years are as follows:

•　　Keep a log of your ADHD symptoms for three months—chart when you have symptoms and when they worsen during your cycle. See if you can find a pattern. Recent studies have found a variation from woman to woman. Symptoms can be as different as having heightened symptoms only one or two days of the month, whereas others have symptoms that get worse for ten days or more during the luteal phase.

•　　Medication can also help. Using a low-dose anti-anxiety or depressant up to two days before your period can help manage the highs and lows of emotions. Other women have found that increasing the dose of medication a few days before their symptoms heighten can help a balanced kick in. There are many ways that medication can help. Talk with your doctor or mental health professional to discuss your options. Do not change your dose without speaking to a doctor or mental health professional.

Pregnancy

During childbirth, hormone levels are incredibly out of whack. With pregnancy, your placenta will produce extra hormones to nourish itself and stimulate other glands, such as your thyroid and adrenal, which produce even more hormones (McCarthy & Novotni, "Women, Hormones, and ADHD," 2022). As your levels expand, you may begin to feel exhausted, have mood swings, and experience anxiety. However, when your estrogen levels kick in and increase again (usually after the first trimester), you should start feeling better—even if you have ADHD.

However, it may take a few days or a week to get your mood leveled out with each new trimester. And, after your child is born, hormone levels drop again. This drop can lead to postpartum depression and mood swings with any new mom, but women with ADHD are more prone to depression.

You and your doctor can evaluate your mood fluctuations in the months leading up to your due date. Keep track of everything you can, including how you react during each trimester shift, after you have the baby and how things are going when you are breastfeeding. There may be some issues with taking ADHD stimulants while breastfeeding, so you may have to rely on other help. However, certain antidepressant medications are safe, even while pregnant. Talk with your doctor about this to determine what is the best course of action for you.

Hormonal changes are unique to ADHD symptoms. You and your ADHD team of medical professionals know what is best for you. Some women have found that while pregnant or breastfeeding, going off their medication helped them function better due to the many hormone shifts of pregnancy.

Interestingly, hormonal changes during pregnancy can improve your ADHD symptoms. However, the hormonal benefits may be counterbalanced by the stress of a new infant, caring for other young children, pregnancy, and work. So it is an unusual kind of balancing act.

Perimenopause and Menopause

If you are a woman who has just landed in menopause or is perimenopausal, you will also have had hormonal shifts.

The average age of menopause is fifty-one, but many other things can trigger this change in women. If you have a full hysterectomy or have genetics that inspire perimenopausal symptoms, these can transition your hormones into chaos when you have ADHD.

This fluctuation happens because your estrogen levels will drop by roughly sixty-five percent between the onslaught of menopause. This decline can last up to ten years and is also part of perimenopause. The loss of your estrogen will lead to a reduction of dopamine and serotonin levels in your brain.

When you lose a steady and healthy stream of these hormones, you can become moody, sad, exhausted, and irritable. Your thoughts can also become fuzzy and lapse in your memory (McCarthy & Novotni, "Women, Hormones, and ADHD," 2022).

Quinn discusses this as the type of cognitive energy. She states, "Given a brain that, in effect, has less cognitive energy, to begin with, it can be especially hard for women with ADHD at this time in their life to concentrate and to make good decisions (2002)."

Solutions are similar to reproductive and puberty stages of life. However, they also include oral contraceptives, improving brain function, and balancing hormone levels. Once your period stops, you may be put on hormone-replacement therapy or can talk to your doctor about how this process can help you. Hormone-replacement therapy can happen for a few years. When you are on this type of therapy, Quinn explains that women on this type of therapy have been found to perform better on "cognitive testing, as well as on memory and reasoning-skills tests (2002)."

Many women do well with an estrogen-only treatment for up to four months and then follow it with ten days of progesterone.

It is important to seek the best course of treatment throughout each stage of your life. While ADHD symptoms can be managed, shifts in your hormones exacerbate symptoms and seem to come out of nowhere. Knowing what your body is going through by educating yourself about ADHD compared to symptoms and mood swings can help you keep up with anything that may throw a wrench in your normal behavior.

You can keep lists of your medications, chart your symptoms, be in touch with what is going on with your body, and continue to include medical and mental health professionals in your treatment. These actions will help you stay on track and prevent you from being blindsided (McCarthy & Novotni, Women, Hormones, and ADHD, 2022).

Exercise Eighteen: Are Your Hormones Out of Whack?

There are a few ways to track your hormones besides charting and journaling yourself.

You can use a saliva test, give a blood sample to an endocrinologist, do a urine test, and take a blood spot test. Several of these tests are kits you can purchase and take at home. However, you may still need a doctor's help to review them.

If you are interested in keeping track of your hormones with a journal, you can build a period tracker by taking the next three to six months and writing about it. Keep your layout simple, so it is easy for you to read and remember.

You can create a physical chart in a notebook with month and date columns. Questions to answer in your journal are as follows:

- List period symptoms. Think about your symptoms, including cravings, pain, mood shifts, etc.

- Track your mood during each cycle. You can do this with simple icons, emoji stickers, or something similar.

- Create a list of self-care tips you can use when feeling low. Having a list of ideas about hygiene, healthy food, meditation, relaxation, and more will help you when you might forget (Dua, 2022).

- Find out when ovulation is and record those dates. You can find this out with a home kit or with the help of a doctor.

- If you have sex, make sure to record the dates. This is a good practice to have even if you are not trying to get pregnant.

If you prefer technology because of notifications and reminders, there are many types of apps for your phone that you can download and use.

Exercise Nineteen: Finding Natural Ways to Help with Hormones

While you can keep track of your hormone swings, you can also find healthy, non-medical ways to keep your hormone levels on track. These methods can include getting proper sleep, good self-care rituals, mindfulness, exercise, and food. Below is a list of helpful tips to find better cooking methods and some ideas to help keep yourself balanced when your hormones and symptoms intermix.

Tips to Follow

Eating clean, whole foods is not the only way to keep your hormone levels in check. Read below for some other tips to help yourself out.

- **Get your protein**—food is essential to helping your body work well. To ensure it works at its highest capacity, ensure you are eating enough protein at each meal. Protein provides crucial amino acids that your body is unable to make. Protein also helps produce hormones called peptides. Endocrine glands make peptides with the help of amino acids. With enough peptides, you will have a good metabolism, appetite, stress management, growth, and reproduction. Try for a minimum of twenty to thirty grams of protein a day.

- **Exercise is important**—not only does exercise burn excess ADHD energy and produce chemicals to help you think more clearly, but it also encourages strong hormonal health. Physical activity improves blood flow to your muscles and increases sensitivity in hormone receptors, which helps reduce insulin levels and fights against possible insulin resistance.

- **Give yourself good gut health**—the gut microbiome (the ecology of your gut) modulates insulin resistance and how full you feel. This area also regulates hormones with over 100 trillion good bacteria. These bacteria can produce many metabolites, which can affect hormone health in a positive or negative way. Pump your body up with pro- and prebiotics to ensure you have healthy bacteria in your gut.

- **Lower your sugars**—not all sugars are bad, but minimizing your sugar intake, especially refined sugar, corn syrup, agave, etc., can severely increase your energy levels and regulate your hormones to a healthy place. Long-term use of any of the items above can promote insulin resistance and make it harder for you to lose weight, eat right, and take care of your hormonal health.

- **Stress Reduction**—lowering your stress levels will revive your hormones in wonderful ways. When your body goes through increased amounts of long-term stress, your cortisol levels will spike and continue to produce until the stress dissipates. However, chronic stress can confuse your system and impair feedback, making your body unsure of what hormones it needs to work properly.

- **Sleep tight**—if you are not getting enough restorative sleep, no amount of healthy food or working out will help your hormones. In fact, poor sleep is linked to imbalances in many hormones like cortisol, ghrelin, HGH, and leptin (Cooper et al., 2018; Lang, 2022).

Conclusion

Depending on the hormone levels within your body, tips, tricks, and food changes can help you level the playing field between medicine, ADHD, and hormones. These items can help you reduce stress, boost your energy, and help you think more clearly.

Taking notes and tracking your menstrual cycles with mood and ADHD symptoms can also help you figure out when you need the most work in what areas.

Reviewing this section will help keep you on top of any emotional regulations, rejection sensitivity, and hormonal issues that may arise in the future. The more you can build self-awareness, the easier time you will have to find a solution to the issue.

The next chapter will discuss more about cleaning, organizing, and decluttering your ADHD lifestyle.

CHAPTER FIVE

Cleaning, Organizing, & Decluttering

What does your home look like?

Do you live in an environment where papers are strewn about, dirty dishes are piled in your sink, and food sits in your refrigerator rotting and forgotten about? If this sounds familiar, you are not alone.

We all struggle to keep our places and spaces clean, especially when busy. If kids are involved, keeping a clean house after they start crawling is nearly impossible. If there is an issue of chronic messiness and disorganization, ADHD makes cleaning and organizing even harder (Davis & Hill, 2022).

Besides hyperactivity, ADHD is synonymous with disorganization and planning. Although, honestly, it is not because of anything you have done. Planning, organizing, and cleaning are all part of executive function, and as discussed in Chapter Three, executive dysfunction is caused by a disconnect between the communication synapses in your brain. When these circuits miscommunicate, they will affect the main skills driven by the executive function.

The three main deficits with executive dysfunction involve self-motivation, planning and problem solving, and non-verbal working memory (Barkley & Novotni, 2022). If you have issues with any of these things, remembering to motivate yourself to clean and plan for decluttering your home can be an issue for anyone with ADHD.

Many women have reported not having people over to their homes because they are embarrassed about how it looks. They worry they do not fit the "good" housekeeper role, like so many other women do—another downfall of a patriarchal society. Instead of focusing on cleaning, you may throw your energy into buying things (especially if you have impulsive-hyperactive ADHD) to put around the house to look nice, which only encourages more clutter.

You may have days where you can throw yourself into cleaning, but it can quickly get overwhelming when you realize just how much you have to clean. Plus, if you get distracted by a few things here and there, you may forget entirely that your focus is to clean the house.

If you feel you are ready to flip your neurodivergent brain on its side and conquer the stereotypical ADHD idea that no one with the disorder can live an organized life, read through the section below.

However, before you start, follow the next few tips to eliminate the pressure to be "clean."

1. Take each project one at a time.

2. Break this project into chunks.

3. Use a timer—set it for ten or fifteen minutes to start. Clean for that amount of time and go do something else.

4. Try this practice every day.

5. Build a SMART goal list and create some SMART goals.

   a. Specific

   b. Measurable

   c. Achievable

   d. Realistic

   e. Timely

The worst thing you can do to yourself is put pressure on the idea of decluttering, cleaning, and organizing. Eliminate words like "should" and "have to" from your cleaning vocabulary. Do not say that your house will "never" be dirty again. Strike these absolute terms to avoid adding that extra stress to a situation. Unrealistic expectations will only set you up for failure, knocking you down. You deserve to keep up and get the life you want. If cleaning, organizing, and decluttering your house is part of that goal, then it is time to start.

The Problem With Clutter & How to Organize

Many problems come with clutter and disorganization. While some issues are innocuous (but frustrating), like losing your keys, glasses, television remote, etc., others can be pretty big, like forgetting appointments, misplacing important documents, and losing bills that need to be paid.

One of the most important steps, if not the most crucial, is to separate yourself from the mess. You are not lazy, dirty, or unclean. Realize that it is not your fault, it is merely the way your brain developed, and you can do things to correct it. Many women with ADHD have this symptom, and it has been noted that many women feel lonely or like an oddity when they just haven't found the best way to work with their brains.

Our book, "Women with ADHD," discusses the emotional calculations that cleaning takes. We say:

"Cleaning with ADHD requires an emotional and logical preparation to begin the task. Once you start, you must follow through with the ideas and complete them. This mental stimulation is exactly the opposite of what an ADHD brain does.

Just because this type of planning works against the ADHD mind does not mean that you will never live in a home that is clean and free of any clutter. However unrealistic it may seem, you CAN work a cleaning routine into your daily life (Davis & Hill, 2022)."

That is great if you are already on a behavioral plan and moving forward. Suppose you have gotten on medication and can think and function with clearer intentions. That is amazing. Alternatively, if you are in the beginning stages of your ADHD education, that is wonderful too. You can always learn more no matter what stage you are in the ADHD process.

Exercise Twenty: Your Umbrella Goals

After you have separated yourself from the clutter and the disorganization, you can set a goal. What would you like it to be? Your cleaning goal can be to get rid of excess clutter in your home, you can have a desire to find important objects with ease, or you can just set your intentions to improve the space you live in.

Think of this goal as the open part of an umbrella. Everything you want to put under the "big" goal will have to do with your main goal. For instance, if you want to improve your living space, you will add other tiers under the umbrella goal and will continue to chunk everything together until they are manageable pieces for your life.

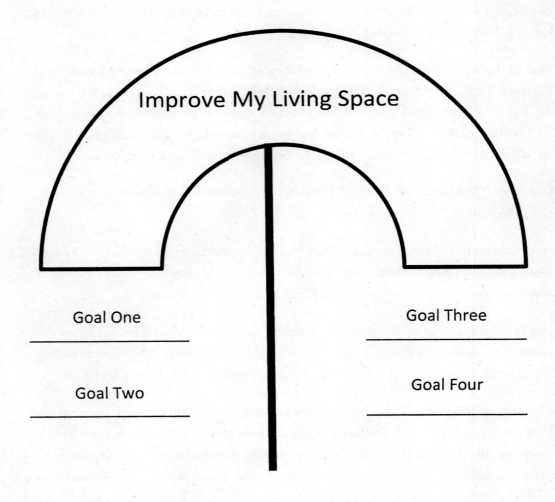

Improve My Living Space

Goal One
_____

Goal Three
_____

Goal Two
_____

Goal Four
_____

Each goal you have under your main goal will be broken down. If you have four goals of "improving my living space," think about what it will look like.

Example Umbella Goal

- Goal One—Keep the kitchen clean.

  - Rinse the dishes right after use and put them in the dishwasher (15 minutes).

  - Run the dishwasher at least once a day.

  - Clean the dishwasher out each day (10 minutes).

  - Wipe down counters every day (5 minutes).

  - Sweep the floor with a broom every other day (15 minutes).

    - Choose two days.

    - Goal Two—Keep the bedroom clean.

  - Make bed every day (3 minutes).

  - Dust dressers, etc., once a week (15 minutes).

  - Vacuum once a week (30 minutes).

  - Put all clothes away (15 minutes).

  - Do laundry once a week.

    - Choose a day.

  - Take out any non-relevant items from the bedroom.

    - List items not relevant for sleeping, resting or getting ready for the day.

- Goal Three—pets.

  - Clean cat litter daily (7 minutes).

- Pick the time before/after work.

- Have kids do it after school.

o Pick up dog poop daily (7 minutes).

- Pick time.

o Take a dog for a walk every day (45 minutes).

- Pick time.

o Clean out birdcage every week (15 minutes).

- Pick a day to do this.

o Feed pets every day at a certain time (5 minutes).

- Pick time.

o Give them water every day at a certain time (5 minutes).

- Pick time.

- Goal Four—get rid of clutter.

  o Start in the living room.

  - Clean one corner of the room a day for fifteen minutes.

  - Put things in boxes to donate.

- Take boxes to the donation bin and pick a deadline.

  - If I have not used or seen it in six months, it is time to donate it or throw it away.

  - Get a bin for extra blankets, pillows, etc.

- Set a deadline to wash, fold, and store these.

- Dust shelves (15 minutes).

- Sweep floors (15 minutes).

- Organize pictures, videos, music, etc., (45 minutes).

○ Go to the bathroom.

- Clean one area daily for fifteen minutes until the entire bathroom is clutter-free.

- Clear away old medications, nail polish, makeup, hair supplies, cleaning products, etc.

- Put items in bags to be thrown out.

- Dispose of old cleaning products appropriately.

  - Clean toilet (10 minutes).

  - Clean bathtub/shower (15 minutes).

  - Clean off counter space and leave only toothbrushes and hand soap on the counter. Everything else gets put away in the cabinet or closet.

  - Wash or sweep the rug/floor (20-30 minutes).

  - Put a fresh hand towel out once a week unless you need to do it sooner.

- Pick a day.

- Add a dirty hand towel to the laundry.

Now It is Your Turn: Place your goal at the top of the list. Fill in the rest of the information in the goals below. Once you complete this list, figure out what goal you want to begin with first, and make sure to write down how long each task is expected to take. That way, you can set a timer for the tasks in the beginning and get yourself into the best practice possible.

Main goal:

_____

- Goal One:

  _____

  - Task_____(time_____)
    - subtask_____(time_____)
    - subtask_____(time_____)
    - subtask_____(time_____)
  - Task_____(time_____)
    - subtask_____(time_____)
    - subtask_____(time_____)
    - subtask_____(time_____)
  - Task_____(time_____)
    - subtask_____(time_____)
    - subtask_____(time_____)
    - subtask_____(time_____)
  - Task_____(time_____)
    - subtask_____(time_____)
    - subtask_____(time_____)
    - subtask_____(time_____)

- Goal Two:

  _____

- ○ Task_____(time_____)
  - ■ subtask_____(time_____)
  - ■ subtask_____(time_____)
  - ■ subtask_____(time_____)
- ○ Task_____(time_____)
  - ■ subtask_____(time_____)
  - ■ subtask_____(time_____)
  - ■ subtask_____(time_____)
- ○ Task_____(time_____)
  - ■ subtask_____(time_____)
  - ■ subtask_____(time_____)
  - ■ subtask_____(time_____)
- ○ Task_____(time_____)
  - ■ subtask_____(time_____)
  - ■ subtask_____(time_____)
  - ■ subtask_____(time_____)

- ● Goal Three: _____
  - ○ Task_____(time_____)
    - ■ subtask_____(time_____)
    - ■ subtask_____(time_____)
    - ■ subtask_____(time_____)

- ○ Task_____(time_____)

  - ■ subtask_____(time_____)

  - ■ subtask_____(time_____)

  - ■ subtask_____(time_____)

- ○ Task_____(time_____)

  - ■ subtask_____(time_____)

  - ■ subtask_____(time_____)

  - ■ subtask_____(time_____)

- ○ Task_____(time_____)

  - ■ subtask_____(time_____)

  - ■ subtask_____(time_____)

  - ■ subtask_____(time_____)

- ● Goal Four:

  - ○ Task_____(time_____)

    - ■ subtask_____(time_____)

    - ■ subtask_____(time_____)

    - ■ subtask_____(time_____)

  - ○ Task_____(time_____)

    - ■ subtask_____(time_____)

    - ■ subtask_____(time_____)

    - ■ subtask_____(time_____)

- ○ Task_____(time_____)

  - ■ subtask_____(time_____)

  - ■ subtask_____(time_____)

  - ■ subtask_____(time_____)

- ○ Task_____(time_____)

  - ■ subtask_____(time_____)

  - ■ subtask_____(time_____)

  - ■ subtask_____(time_____)

A Home that fits your ADHD

Look around your home. Do you see clutter?

You might not recognize that the big piles of paper stashed in the corner of your living room or the kitchen counter filled with utensils, tchotchkes, and boxed foods are clutter. You might think, "If I can see the floor, my home is clean (Davis & Hill, 2022)."

That is normal for ADHD.

The problem happens when your peripheral vision decides that the clutter is too overwhelming to look at, and you go "clutter-blind." Just because you can see the floor in your home does not mean that your cleaning habits are up to snuff or that your house is clean.

To start a clutter-free life, you will have to look at most of the things in your house. It turns out that you can get rid of most of them.

Thinking of throwing away anything may give you heart palpitations. Nothing bad will happen, even if it seems like a bad idea. You are going to try to do things. It will feel awkward and a bit uncomfortable, like wearing a dress that makes you look weird, or puting on a new, brighter lipstick shade when you are used to going neutral. It does not mean that you will always feel uncomfortable. It means that you need to get used to them. It is time to stand out. Wear that dress. Put on that lipstick. Create a clutter-free space for yourself.

A clean, clutter-free environment means a cleaner and less cluttered mind.

Knowing what to throw out and what to keep may sound overwhelming, but ask yourself this: Would taking care of a specific item in the way it was meant to be taken care of be worth your time and effort?

If you answer this question with "yes," keep it. If you answer "no," you know what to do: donate it or throw it away. There are many people who may not have what you do and may need it. Always consider donating if the object is in good condition and you know it can get love and use somewhere else.

You will probably answer "no" more often than "yes." This honesty will help you cut down on having too much clutter faster than you realize. The less you have, the less time there will be to keep it organized and clean (Cantrell, 2022).

Exercise Twenty-One: What and Where is Your Clutter?

You must take off the clutter blinds and look at each room. What do you see? Can you make a list of items that look like they could be cluttered, even if you are sure?

- Dead plants

- Dirty or broken trinkets & tchotchkes

- Piles of paper

- Cardboard boxes from online orders

- Food wrappers

- Books

- Cans

- Bottles

- Crafting supplies that you are always meaning to use

- Holiday decorations to be put away

- Picture frames that need hung up

- Trophies, Awards, Certificates

- Pet supplies

- Cooking supplies

- Body, hygiene, & makeup products

- Receipts

- Fast food leftovers

- Dirty paper towels

- Old sponges

- Computer supplies

- Cleaning supplies

- Shoes

- And more

You can fill out the spaces below if you need to list the clutter in each room. The above examples can provide a good foundation to know what to look for, but it can be anything from dryer lint and sheets to clothes and accessories strewn about the floor.

- Living Room: _____

  o Corner One

    - _____

    - _____

    - _____

    - _____

    - _____

  o Corner Two

    - _____

    - _____

    - _____

- ■ _____
- ■ _____

○ Corner Three

- ■ _____
- ■ _____
- ■ _____
- ■ _____
- ■ _____

○ Corner Four

- ■ _____
- ■ _____
- ■ _____
- ■ _____
- ■ _____

- ● Bathroom: _____

○ Corner One

- ■ _____
- ■ _____
- ■ _____
- ■ _____

- ■ _____

- ○   Corner Two

  - ■ _____

  - ■ _____

  - ■ _____

  - ■ _____

  - ■ _____

- ○   Corner Three

  - ■ _____

  - ■ _____

  - ■ _____

  - ■ _____

  - ■ _____

- ○   Corner Four

  - ■ _____

  - ■ _____

  - ■ _____

  - ■ _____

  - ■ _____

- ●   Bedroom One: _____

○   Corner One

- ■ _____
- ■ _____
- ■ _____
- ■ _____
- ■ _____

○   Corner Two

- ■ _____
- ■ _____
- ■ _____
- ■ _____
- ■ _____

○   Corner Three

- ■ _____
- ■ _____
- ■ _____
- ■ _____
- ■ _____

○   Corner Four

- ■ _____

- ▪ _____

- ▪ _____

- ▪ _____

- ▪ _____

- ● Bedroom Two: _____

  ○ Corner One

    - ▪ _____

    - ▪ _____

    - ▪ _____

    - ▪ _____

    - ▪ _____

  ○ Corner Two

    - ▪ _____

    - ▪ _____

    - ▪ _____

    - ▪ _____

    - ▪ _____

  ○ Corner Three

    - ▪ _____

    - ▪ _____

- ■ _____
- ■ _____
- ■ _____

  ○ Corner Four

  - ■ _____
  - ■ _____
  - ■ _____
  - ■ _____
  - ■ _____

- ● Bedroom Three: _____

  ○ Corner One

  - ■ _____
  - ■ _____
  - ■ _____
  - ■ _____
  - ■ _____

  ○ Corner Two

  - ■ _____
  - ■ _____
  - ■ _____

- ■ _____
- ■ _____

- ○ Corner Three

  - ■ _____
  - ■ _____
  - ■ _____
  - ■ _____
  - ■ _____

- ○ Corner Four

  - ■ _____
  - ■ _____
  - ■ _____
  - ■ _____
  - ■ _____

- ● Kitchen: _____

- ○ Corner One

  - ■ _____
  - ■ _____
  - ■ _____
  - ■ _____

- ■ _____

○ Corner Two

- ■ _____

- ■ _____

- ■ _____

- ■ _____

- ■ _____

○ Corner Three

- ■ _____

- ■ _____

- ■ _____

- ■ _____

- ■ _____

○ Corner Four

- ■ _____

- ■ _____

- ■ _____

- ■ _____

- ■ _____

● Extra Room: _____

- ○ **Corner One**

  - ■ _____

  - ■ _____

  - ■ _____

  - ■ _____

  - ■ _____

- ○ **Corner Two**

  - ■ _____

  - ■ _____

  - ■ _____

  - ■ _____

  - ■ _____

- ○ **Corner Three**

  - ■ _____

  - ■ _____

  - ■ _____

  - ■ _____

  - ■ _____

- ○ **Corner Four**

  - ■ _____

- ■ _____
- ■ _____
- ■ _____
- ■ _____

- ● Extra Room: _____

○ Corner One

- ■ _____
- ■ _____
- ■ _____
- ■ _____
- ■ _____

○ Corner Two

- ■ _____
- ■ _____
- ■ _____
- ■ _____
- ■ _____

○ Corner Three

- ■ _____
- ■ _____

- _____
- _____
- _____

○   Corner Four

- _____
- _____
- _____
- _____
- _____

Exercise Twenty-Two: Purging Your Clutter

Once you have an idea of what your clutter is, you can start to purge the clutter.

Ask yourself a few things:

- **What are my target areas?** You can pinpoint these by finding spots in your home that gather the most mess. Remember you live in this space and know what works best for you (or do not be afraid to try new things). Find what feels the most comfortable and set that as your standard.

- **Where can I clean to make things easier on myself**—Where do you spend the most time? Are you in the kitchen, living room, office, etc.?

- **What is your biggest problem area**—Do you have too many shoes? Are you finding that you have piles of paper everywhere?

- **Where do you want to start**—Sometimes, cleaning the biggest area will be the most overwhelming. Pick where you are most comfortable starting and go for it.

You can set a timer so you do not feel trapped by clutter and stick to it, so you do not get distracted or become hyperfocused and burn out.

Below is a list to help you start on your clutter-free journey. Check some ideas that seem like they would work best for you and try them out (Cantrell, 2022; Davis & Hill, 2022).

- **Clothes**—Do your clothes get tossed on the floor? Over a bench? Left in the bathroom?

- Add hooks to your doors to hang the clothes you plan on wearing again before washing.

For example, hanging things like pajamas on a hook can alleviate the stress of having clothes build up on the floor or save you from looking for them when you are getting ready for bed.

- Keep a laundry basket in these areas if you do not wear clothes a second time, but they are thrown over the floor in your bathroom, laundry room, or bedroom. Take (and keep) the lid off to make it even easier.

If you have issues with throwing clothes on the floor, even after they are clean, dedicate one or two baskets to clean clothes only. Keep clean clothes in these baskets until you are ready to fold them—but still, make folding your clothes a priority in your routine.

- **Kitchen**—What are your biggest problem areas in the kitchen? Are the counters cleaned off? Do you have coffee accessories thrown everywhere? Do fruit and spices get tossed into the same place?

- To solve this problem, get baskets. Lots of baskets. Do this after you clear the counters and tables off.

Keep your coffee supplies in one basket. Your fruit in another. Your spices in a third, and so on. Get a basket for every item you have put away. Give each basket of items a specific place on your counter or table.

For example, keep fruit near the snack drawers or other places you have food.

- Use labels to help you remember what is where and what to use.

- Add a list of items you need to buy each time you run out. They have some great ones that are also magnets for you to stick to your refrigerator.

- **Desk**—Do you have papers that pile up everywhere? Can you not find the proper tools needed to complete a task?

- Get yourself a few filing shelves with no lids. Keep two on your desk—one for "to-read" items and one for "read" items.

Put your pencils, paperclips, rubber bands, post-it notes, etc., in baskets.

- Get an open shelving unit to add everything to. Clean it off every week or twice a month.

Throw away things you do not need, file what you need, and keep a color-coded system for each shelf (blue means bills, green means cleaning supplies, etc.)

- Get a large calendar to add your deadlines. Set the calendar on your desk, so it is always in view (Cantrell, 2022; Davis & Hill, 2022).

- **Trash**—Where does most trash wind up?

- Put a garbage can close to that area. Do not hide it, do not keep a lid on it—keep it near where garbage piles up and make it easy for yourself to throw things away instead of leaving them on the floor, table, counter, etc.

For example, if you eat snacks in front of the TV, put a can next to the couch to throw the wrappers into the garbage can as soon as you eat the snack.

- Set an alarm each day, or twice a day if needed, then stand up from your area and pick up any trash that has accrued (Cantrell, 2022; Davis & Hill, 2022).

Tackle each corner of each room one day a week for a set amount of time until each area has been decluttered. If you use fifteen minutes a day, that is a short burst of time that you set for yourself and can be manageable. Unless you find decluttering your space a Zen experience, stay away from trying to do two-hour chunks or more. You are trying to create a healthy balance for yourself.

Clutter does not have to go away all at once. The important thing with this practice is building a clutter-free environment and learning to have healthy cleaning habits.

Exercise Twenty-Three: Chore Charts and Rewards Lists

The purpose of creating a chore chart and reward list is simple. You will see it. With ADHD, you may have an issue called "object permanence." This idea is similar to, but not exactly, the object permanence we learn as children when we play "peek-a-boo."

If something is out of sight with the ADHD brain, it may be out of mind. That does not mean you do not realize it is gone completely or forever, but it does mean that until you see it again, you will forget it is even there.

There are many ways to create chore charts and reward lists. One example of each is below. If you have a better idea that will suit your lifestyle and start you on the visualization journey, feel free to use it! See the example below, you can check off each day you do the chore and cross out, or X the days you did not have to.

Daily Chores

	M	Tu	W	Th	F	Sa	Su
Wash the dishes/dishwasher	😀	😠	☐	🤩	😣	☐	🤓

The example above shows that emoji are for more fun touch, but you can use anything that your heart fancies.

The other chart is for rewards, which are completely up to you. Make a list of items you want to do, buy, eat, play, etc. Then set appropriate rewards once you have finished decluttering a room, or hit four out of seven days on your chore chart.

Make a list like the one below. Don't forget to add what you have to do to get the reward!

Reward List

	Reward	M	Tu	W	Th	F	Sa	Su
Did chores five days in a row	Movie Night	✹	✹	✹	✹	✹	✹	✹
I got all four corners of clutter cleaned in the living room	Buy a new item							
Got the first floor cleaned	Go to the spa							
Did chores for two weeks in a row	Go to dinner at your favorite restaurant. Order whatever you want.							

After you have used a reward, make sure to reset it. Also, keep a list handy of things you would like rewards for. Entertainment, dining, outdoor experiences, and bath time can all be used. Take the things you love to do the most and leverage them to help you clean, declutter, and make your space more ADHD breathable.

Conclusion

Learning how to declutter, clean, and organize your life is going to help your ADHD situate itself in a new and exciting way. You'll start to be able to see the benefits of having a clean space, being organized in each part of your life, and enjoying the rewards that come your way.

Chapter Six will give you a few ideas how to work with ADHD, have friends, build a career, and keep healthy financial practices.

CHAPTER SIX

ADHD & Relationships

Social life, career, and financial health are all vital elements for living a more focused-driven life. When something is out of whack, you can work on it easily, but if everything seems as though it piles up, falls over, swirls around, and creates chaos, these things may seem as though they are impossible to touch. They are not, but first, you need to know where to start.

Women with ADHD tend to be socially isolated more because they feel as though they have a weakened understanding of how to be social. You do not, but that is the consensus in research and evidence found in studies (Novotni, 2022).

Many women responded that they feel exposed and vulnerable in the areas below:

- No social connections with acquaintances, business associates, and friends.

- How to master multi-tasking by switching between family, home, work, and friends.

- An inability to ask for help or assert their news.

- Feeling sadness due to a lack of positive social interaction leads to isolation (Novotni, 2022).

You can avoid staying in an isolated frame of mind, but you will have to do a few things and help shake yourself out of those places where you are stuck.

Exercise Twenty-Four: Tips and Tricks for Stepping out of Social Isolation

- **Do not be too hard on yourself.** No one learns social skills in school. There are

269

no "do's" and "don'ts" of how to behave in situations, but society tells each other that we should know what to do and when to do it. If you come across people like this, know that you can create healthy boundaries and do not need to develop a deeper friendship with them. We are all flawed, and anyone who says differently is lying to themselves.

- **Focus on people who will give you honest, kind, and unconditional feedback.** Although it may be hard to ask someone what social skills you need to improve on if you are genuine in your desire to change and approach them with an open mind, you can give yourself an amazing opportunity for growth and change (Davis & Hill, 2022).

- **Multi-task your relationships**. Luckily, ADHD allows you to be a stellar multi-tasker. Although it can be hard with the pressures life puts on you, make sure to spend some time with your friends. If you have to carve out time purposefully, you must do that. With everything you have going on, you will drain yourself easily if you do not make time for yourself and some people who do not rely on you (aka friends!) for everything.

- **Women do not need to "have it all," "do it all," and "be it all."** That is way too much pressure to put on yourself, and if people in your life are making you feel that way, then you can reassess those healthy boundaries. Delegation and self-care are the right way to have a healthy mental state. If you have children and a spouse, everyone living in the family can have tasks.

- **Learn how to assert yourself, even if you hate conflict**. You are always going to come across things that are uncomfortable or even those you downright hate. You may be in the practice of pushing things down or talking yourself into being the person to blame, but that is not the case. It shows healthy boundaries and confidence in yourself when you know how to say, "I do not like this." Try to find friends and partners whom you can learn to ask for what you want without judgment or friction. If you are afraid, you can always precursor that information by saying, "I am very uncomfortable, but I would like to talk to you."

- **Understand that ADHD is going to give you strong feelings**. Remember that you are not only a woman with ADHD but also a woman with feelings. People in your life may tell you that you react strongly about things. These actions are okay, but make sure to assess them with a mental health professional to see if they are associated with emotional dysregulation or just mere feelings you feel (Davis & Hill, 2022).

The Challenges of Friendship

Exercise Twenty-Five: What Type of Friend are You?

It's almost redundant to say that ADHD has a laundry list of items that infringe on your life, but it touches on your social life too. Maintaining healthy friendships where both people put the relationship may heighten some of your ADHD symptoms without you even realizing it. Think about what kind of friend you are, do you feel any of the items listed below? Check the boxes that sound like you and add

in some extra ones in the space if they aren't listed.

- Feeling Overwhelmed

- Getting Bored

- Inconsistency With Friendships

- Poor Memory

- Your Self-Esteem

- Your Depression & Anxiety

- Lack of Friends Equals a Lack of Acceptance.

- The Shame of Friendship.

- Reciprocating is Difficult.

- Time Issues

- Your Phone is Your Lifeline.

- Your Thoughts May Not Cooperate (Broadbent, 2022).

- _____

- _____

- _____

- _____

Once you figure out what type of issues you may have with friendships, review the ADHD symptoms and see if any of the actions in the different ADHD kinds sound similar to how you have treated your friends:

Women with Hyperactive-Impulsive ADHD will:

- Get bored easily

- Interrupt others

- Ignore social rules

- Blurt out negative criticism

- Control the conversations

- Focus the conversation on themselves

- Enhance their stimulation level with substances

- End frustrating relationships.

Women with Inattentive ADHD will:

- Be overwhelmed by social and emotional demands.

- Avoid impromptu social gatherings.

- Have anxiety in unfamiliar environments (especially with many people).

- Second-guess and censor their feelings and responses if they feel conflict coming.

- Create flaws to have others avoid them, so they do not have to avoid others.

- Label mistakes as character flaws.

- Assume everyone will reject or criticize them (Davis & Hill, 2022).

Does any of this sound like you? Can you think of ways to work with them or challenge your ideas? Do you think you may be in denial of what kind of friend you are?

Think about it and write those thoughts in your journal or the space below.

_____

_____

_____

_____

_____

_____

_____

_____

_____

_____

_____

_____

_____

_____

_____

_____

_____

_____

_____

_____

_____

_____

_____

_____

_____

_____

_____

_____

_____

_____

_____

_____

_____

Exercise Twenty-Six: Some Social Strategies to Consider

See the questions below. Answer them in the best way you know how to. If you are unsure, write your thoughts, then go over them with a trusted friend, partner, counselor, or mental health professional.

- How can you accept yourself fully? Finding a way to look at yourself with respect, value, and love will attract some amazing people. What are a few ways to help yourself?

_____

_____

_____

_____

_____

_____

- How can technology help your friendships? With everything that technology offers, including notifications, alarms, and reminders, how could you use your smartphone to help you keep in touch with your people? For example, emails, texts, and calendars are a great start.

_____

_____

_____

_____

_____

_____

- How comfortable are you talking about your ADHD? Remember, everyone has flaws, your ADHD does not have to be considered one of them, but the symptoms bring certain challenges to the friendship table. Name some of those items below. If you are not comfortable talking about your ADHD with a certain friend, think about if you are uncomfortable with your ADHD or maybe worried that your friend will not accept you for you. If the response is the latter, you might want to think about distancing yourself from that person.

_____

_____

_____

_____

_____

_____

- Do you know what your ADHD triggers are? Your actions, thoughts, and words may seem as though they come out of nowhere when there is a moment of a trigger that could boost your ADHD symptoms. Write some triggers below, what you can do when faced with them, and how you can rebound if you cannot.

_____

_____

_____

_____

_____

_____

- Do you know what activities you like to do most? If you make plans with your friends, think about doing something where you can move around. That would give you the optimal time to burn energy and build bonds with a friend or group of friends. Write some ideas of things you like to do that are active below.

_____

_____

_____

_____

_____

_____

- If you want to reciprocate and host an event at your place, you should! But remember to take things slowly. Start small and work your way up to bigger and better events. Write some ideas below to see how incredible your dinner party, brunch, or game night can be. Remember that everyone is an adult and can bring something to the gathering, do not put everything all on yourself. That is the perfect way to burn out before you start.

_____

_____

_____

_____

_____

_____

Friendly Advice: Cut some slack and give yourself time to transition into new habits. Remember to be flexible with your friends as well as your actions. Although you have ADHD, it should not stop you from remembering that other people's lives, interests, families, feelings, and more are just as important as yours.

When you build strong relationships with others, you will find a vital part of your life that you have missed.

Your Relationship with Romance

ADHD will affect how you look at a partner and how your partner looks at you. While it can be fun and exciting at first, once the shine wears off, you may wonder what to do next, especially if you want to stay in the relationship and develop it into something deeper.

Look at the challenge below. Does this sound like something you have done with a romantic partner? For a woman in a serious relationship, distractions can come from the simplest places. An example taken from CHADD.org goes something like this:

Partner without ADHD: "Hey, hon—do you want to watch a movie?"

Partner with ADHD: "Sure, I will go make popcorn."

- She walks to the kitchen to make popcorn but sees clothes and toys lying on the floor in the den. She picks them up and takes them to her child's room to put them away.

- She sees that her child forgot to put their toothbrush away and left it on their desk. Even though she is annoyed with her child's inability to put things away, she picks them up and takes them to the bathroom (the clothes and toys are forgotten about).

- She realizes it needs to be cleaned up when she gets to the bathroom. She pulls out the cleaning supplies and begins wiping down the counter.

- Her partner starts looking for her throughout the house and finds her cleaning the bathroom. The partner sees her doing other things, popcorn still not made, and believes she never wanted to watch the movie in the first place (CHADD, 2018; Davis & Hill, 2022).

While none of the items above were done intentionally to hurt your partner, the steady stream of distractions allowed the woman with ADHD to lose her way from the original goal of spending romantic time together. The book Women with ADHD states,

"If you are aware of your ADHD and have open communication with your partner about it, this instance might not be a big deal—it might even be expected. However, if your ADHD is undiagnosed, if this type of event happens often, or if you are not transparent with your partner, they may begin to see it as an issue and believe you don't want to spend time with them (Davis & Hill, 2022)."

Exercise Twenty-Seven: Map Out a Distraction Moment

Think about the example above. Does it sound familiar? Write down an instance where this has happened and map out where your distractions took you, plus what time you lost with your partner. If it caused any larger consequences, write that down also. Being aware of your trail of distractions can help you redirect yourself when you recognize what is going on.

Agreed Upon Activity: _____

You get up and go to do something but then find the stream of distractions waiting for you.

What happens?

➔ _____

➔ _____

➔ _____

➔ _____

➔ _____

→ _____
   ___

→ _____

→ _____

→ _____

→ _____

→ _____

→ _____

→ _____

→ _____

How did things end up? _____

Did you get any consequences? _____

What could you have done differently? _____

Some tips to help:

- Talk things out.

- Do things that are interesting to both of you. Do not be afraid to try something new.

- Look at physical intimacy as an opportunity to mutually satisfy one another.

- Find professional help.

Your Relationship with Your Career

Building a career can be a tricky business.

Excuse the pun.

When you have ADHD, finding something that will hold your interest can be hard. If the task or project does not hold your attention, you may wind up quitting more jobs than you can list. Although working in an office seems like a good place to start your career, you may often feel restless or hate the thought of even going in. This may have you develop a work habit of long hours that may keep you staying late into the night or showing up earlier in the morning so you can focus and have quiet time to get work done.

If you hate your job, why do you work there?

You need money.

You cannot just fall into a "perfect" career.

What are some other reasons you work in the job you do?

The great thing about ADHD is that you can work a "pay the bills job" while seeking the job of your dreams. You have enough energy, strength, and creativity to work a full-time job, take care of a home, and pursue something you are passionate about. The most important question you need to ask yourself when thinking about your career is:

What do you really want to do?

Do not worry if you are not sure. There are many ways to find out what is right for you. Suppose you hear a little voice in your head telling you that something you want to do is not possible. Do not listen or tell it off. You are a creative, dynamic, multi-tasking machine. You can do anything (Davis & Hill, 2022).

Once you find the right pieces to your ADHD puzzle, you will be pretty much unstoppable.

Exercise Twenty-Eight: Find Your Chosen Career

Ask yourself the questions below. Answer them accordingly.

- What can you spend hours talking about or researching?

_____

_____

_____

_____

_____

- What would you prefer to do with your weekend time?

_____

_____

_____

_____

_____

- Can you work in a team, or do you choose to work individually?

_____

_____

_____

_____

_____

- Do you like to be in charge? Are you comfortable taking the lead?

_____

_____

_____

_____

_____

- What bothers you the most about people, places, and things (what are your pet peeves) (Davis & Hill, 2022)?

_____

_____

_____

_____

_____

- Do you prefer fast- or slow-paced environments?

_____

_____

_____

_____

- What activities drain you, and which ones excite you?

_____

_____

_____

_____

- What job would you love to do if money wasn't an issue (Davis & Hill, 2022)?

_____

_____

_____

_____

_____

Now that you have a few answers, maybe some of the career ideas below can help grease the wheels of inspiration.

The Best Jobs for ADHD Minds are:

- Artist
- Athlete
- Beautician
- Chef
- Computer technician
- Copy editor
- Daycare worker
- Emergency Medical Technician (EMT), first responder
- Engineer
- Hair Stylist

- High-tech field
- Hospitality management or industry
- Journalist
- Nurse
- Sales representative (not in a call center)
- Small business owner
- Software engineer
- Stage management in the theater
- Teacher (Sheppard, 2021)

Do any of these sound like something you would like to do? If so, why don't you journal out a plan to get to where you want to be? If not, journal about some subjects you are most passionate about.

Your Relationship with Money

What is your relationship with money?

Do you avoid looking at your checking account?

Do you constantly forget where your bills are?

Are you unaware of how much credit card debt you have?

Are things okay and work well?

What are your money goals?

Exercise Twenty-Nine: What Are Your Goals?

Think about what you'd like your future with money to be. Include short-, mid-, and long-term goals. Make sure to include your partner or spouse if you have one (Davis & Hill, 2022).

Short-term goals examples are: Eat out less, keep financial documents organized, or save a specific amount of money each week.

Mid-term goal examples can be: going on vacation, buying new furniture, paying off one credit card, etc.

Long-term goal examples can be: building college savings or adding to your retirement funds.

Write these items below:

Short-term goals:

_____

_____

_____

_____

_____

_____

_____

_____

_____

_____

Mid-term goals:

_____

_____

_____

_____

_____

_____

_____

Long-term goals:

_____

_____

_____

_____

_____

_____

_____

Once you have a few ideas, you can create a vision board with images of items you would like to purchase in the future, or you can sort out your desired purchases into non-essentials and essential supplies (Davis & Hill, 2022). Answer the questions below to help:

What are the top three to five must-haves on your essential list?

_____

_____

_____

_____

_____

What are your top three to five must-haves on your non-essential list (Davis & Hill, 2022)?

_____

_____

_____

_____

_____

_____

_____

_____

What is your current financial status?

_____

_____

_____

_____

_____

_____

_____

_____

What is stopping you from having a healthy economic life?

_____

_____

_____

_____

_____

_____

_____

Where would you like to see yourself financially in one, three, and five years (Davis & Hill, 2022)?

_____

_____

_____

_____

_____

_____

_____

_____

Finding some problem spots in your spending habits can help you resolve some of the bigger money-related issues you have had. To develop successful money management, you must pay attention to the details. Each goal you set for your financial planning plays a vital role in your financial health.

If you find that you have impulse spending issues, review some tips below from the Women with ADHD companion book and see if they can help you curb your impulses.

Tips for taming your impulses:

- Click 'unsubscribe.' These darn emails send a bunch of sales and specials to your inbox.

- Keep track of what you spend while you shop.

- Learn what your temptations are, and come up with a plan to stay away from them.

- Look for things to do locally that are free or inexpensive.

- Make things a little harder on yourself. Keep the credit cards at home. Bring the lowest amount of money you think you will need.

- Find an amount of time that feels right, like twenty-four hours, and wait to purchase your item. If, after time passes, you have the money and still want the bigger object, then you can buy it.

- Use a shopping list and stick to the items on it. There will be times when you make a list and forget one ingredient for dinner.

- Vulnerability leads to that needed dose of dopamine, and when you are shopping, that can be a super trigger. If you find yourself shopping in an emotional mood, returning to the task later is best when you feel more grounded and focused.

Conclusion

Throughout this chapter, you took a quick pass through your social, career, and financial relationships. While these are not an extensive list of places you can go, they are all good exercise and tips on where you can start. Hopefully, with time, practice, and help from others, you will find yourself getting into a good pattern with friends, romance, and finances. Also, keep looking for the job you are most passionate about. You deserve to love what you do and to do what you love.

The next chapter will discuss health, exercise, and ADHD mind-body tips and tricks.

CHAPTER SEVEN

ADHD, Health & Exercise

Introduction

Treating your body and mind well helps keep your body and mind working in the most efficient way they can. This chapter will discuss a few of those items and give tips and tricks on eating and treating yourself well to be well.

Healthy Eating

Factually, no significant data has connected ADHD with what you eat. However, research indicates that certain foods and vitamins help your brain and body function smoother than without whole foods.

Neurologically, foods rich in protein help build connections between neurotransmitters, which means your brain will have a better foundation for more streamlined communication.

Examples of Protein-Rich Foods

- Beans
- Eggs
- Fish
- Nuts
- Poultry

Examples of Vitamins and Minerals

Zink, iron, and magnesium have been shown to regulate neurotransmitters and level out cognitive differences. Regular incorporation of zinc into your diet will encourage dopamine regulation, calming your brain. Magnesium will refocus and relax your brain, whereas low iron levels have been shown to correlate with cognitive issues (Muhammad, 2022; Davis & Hill, 2022).

Statements about food in the Women with ADHD companion book are as follows:

"Foods high on the Glycemic Index (GI) can release rapid glucose, increasing inattention, hyperactivity, and impulsivity. Processed foods like artificial dyes and white, refined sugars have a poor connection with brain activity. They are generally recommended to steer clear from when you have any sort of neurological disruption.

If you get knowledgeable about reading the labels on your food packages, you'll be able to learn the foods to stay away from and which ones are good for you. Words like: dehydrated cane juice, dextrin, dextrose, high-fructose corn sweetener, maltodextrin, molasses, malt syrup, and sucrose are all code words for sugar (Davis & Hill, 2022; Muhammad, 2022)."

Healthy Foods to Eat

- **Artichokes**—this vegetable supports the function of the liver. The liver detoxes the body, and adding artichokes can boost that process. They are also high in fiber, which promotes lower-hormone levels for when your levels may be riding a little high. When you have higher or too high hormone levels, your body will produce more cortisol and estrogen, which can increase breast chance in certain individuals.

  Foods high in fiber digest slowly so you will feel fuller longer and help you maintain healthy energy levels throughout your day (Azzaro, 2021).

- **Broccoli**—this vegetable is in a group called cruciferous. Broccoli is rich in glucosinolates like kale, cabbage, Brussels sprouts, and cauliflower. This compound helps eliminate and neutralize carcinogens, indole-three-cabriole, and isothiocyanates, which are nutrients to help prevent estrogen-related cancers.

Broccoli is a vegetable high in fiber and assists in removing excess estrogen through bowel movements (Nutrition, 2022).

- **Flaxseeds**—this seed contains lignans, which is a plant-based, estrogen-like substance and weaker than the estrogen that your body makes. The benefits include healthy hormone levels by creating longer luteal phases (the second part of your menstrual cycle), lowering estrogen and testosterone levels, reducing breast pain, and preventing postmenopausal breast cancer.

Flax seeds are also high in fiber (Azzaro, 2021).

Fresh Herbs—aromatic herbs like garlic, ginger and turmeric, basil, oregano, parsley, and thyme are ripe with nutritious phytochemicals that can benefit your health (Azzaro, 2021).

- **Lentils**—like salmon and artichokes, lentils are a slow-burning protein, which means you will feel fuller longer. They are also an amazing source of fiber, protein, and zinc. Lentils can reduce estrogen levels and raise testosterone (Nutrition, 2022).

- **Salmon**—this fish is a good source of omega-three fatty acids and vitamin E, which are great bases for anti-inflammatory healing. Salmon also contains cholesterol. Cholesterol is the main ingredient that helps make hormones. It is a waxy substance in all cells that helps create cholesterol. Although different foods have cholesterol, you will want to eat plenty of food with HDL (high-density lipoproteins) and stay away from LDL (low-density lipoproteins). Low-density lipoproteins leave deposits of plaque in your arteries and create blockages. High-density lipoproteins will carry the plaque out of your arteries (Younkin, 2021).

Because salmon is an anti-inflammatory food, it will help reduce menstrual cramping, lower the production of stress hormones, and help alleviate cortisol levels.

The protein in salmon digest slower than in other food, which means you will have a satisfying feeling for longer after you eat it (Azzaro, 2021).

- **Shrimp and Shellfish**—examples of this food include scallops, clams, and shrimp. This type of seafood has an abundance of good minerals like iodine, zinc, and selenium, which are vital to a properly functioning thyroid. Although in a much lower dose than salmon, these foods also contain many omega-three fatty acids and act as anti-inflammatory.

Shrimp, muscles, scallops, etc., contain EPA, DHA, and tryptophan, which encourage the production of melatonin in the body, a crucial hormone for good sleep (Azzaro, 2021).

- **Sunflower Seeds**—are rich in vitamin E, an antioxidant important to estrogen, and boost progesterone, too (Nutrition, 2022).

- **Sweet Potatoes**—this type of tuber is high in vitamin B6 and helps your body by detoxifying the liver. Any foods that aid by detoxing your liver assists in ridding extra hormones. Chicken, turkey, and spinach are other foods plentiful with vitamin B6 (Nutrition, 2022).

- **Organic Tempeh**—organic soy has positive effects that come from isoflavones. Isoflavones have phytoestrogen properties that help reduce the risk of breast cancer and can increase probiotics when eaten with a fermentation agent (Nutrition, 2022).

For Adrenal Hormones

If you find that you have adrenal fatigue or that it is hyperactive, you can eat some of the food below to help you balance out any issues and give your medication a boost.

- **Almonds** contain healthy fats to help balance blood sugar, support nervous system function, and reduce inflammation.

- **Avocado**—has a spectrum of healthy fats to keep blood sugar levels even and supports proper nervous system functionality. Avocado contains vitamin B5, which helps fight stress (Nutrition, 2022).

- **Bell Peppers**—green, red, yellow, and orange bell peppers are sweet and full of vitamin C. This vitamin is an antioxidant essential to a good functioning adrenal gland. Foods that are high in vitamin C will replenish, reduce stress levels, and give you a nice energy boost.

- **Eggs**—will boost your choline, a vitamin that assists in the production of the neurotransmitter acetylcholine. This vitamin is crucial to helping your brain, nervous system, memory, and development function well. When you buy organic, pasture-raised eggs, you will get a nice dose of omega-three fatty acids, which also aid in reducing inflammation.

- **Kale**—while not in the cruciferous family, kale is a dark, leafy green that provides various nutrients like vitamins K, A, and C. Kale has similar traits to bell peppers as it brings in extra antioxidants to help with stress reduction.

- **Millet**—contains a variety of B vitamins to support the nervous system and reduce stress. It is also whole grain and gluten-free. With extra fiber and magnesium to boot, it will help balance your blood sugar levels.

- **Pumpkin Seeds**—these seeds are rich in magnesium, which works in tandem with vitamins C and B5. This type of seed will lower stress levels and help us relax.

- **Sea Salt**—when you are depleted of the hormone aldosterone, you will crave salt. However, this generally means that your adrenal glands are not working either. When you add sea salt to your food or even a glass of water, you will replenish your levels and bump up the balance in your fluid and blood pressure (Nutrition, 2022).

For Thyroid Hormones

Thyroid issues are a problem that has not been completely figured out due to the complex nature of your thyroid. If it works well, you will not notice a difference, but if it is out of balance, you can become hypo or hyper-. Neither of these thyroid problems is good for your body, and while medication usually is an important part of the healing process, some tests may not show that you have an issue. However, if you notice a drastic change in weight and energy, you could have an imbalance that does not show up on tests. See some helpful food below that can give you a place to start feeling better.

- **Brazil Nuts**—these nuts are ripe with selenium, which is an antioxidant that converts T4 into T3, an active form of a thyroid hormone. T3 is needed for your thyroid to work well, but selenium also produces your gland.

- **Quinoa**—is a seed and a superfood. This seed has a ton of fiber, minerals, and protein. It is a slow-burning food that allows you to feel fuller longer and will help you with constipation which a slow thyroid will bring.

- **Sardines**—this small fish with a sordid reputation is chock-full of B12, selenium, and iodine. These nutrients are all needed to support your thyroid healthily.

- **Seaweed**—is a vegetable of the sea. You may also find it under other names like arame, dulse, hijiki, kombu, nori, wakame, and more. Seaweed is a great place to find iodine, a vital mineral in the production of thyroid hormones.

- **Spinach**—is amazing vegetation that helps enhance thyroid function and hormones and boosts energy. Spinach is rich in iron, B vitamins, and fiber (Nutrition, 2022).

Exercise

When thinking about exercise, it's best to find something that you like to do. If you're not a huge fan of exercise, start with walking because exercise is crucial to help your ADHD brain to "focus, burn energy, and relieve yourself of some of those peskier symptoms like impulsivity and inattention (Davis & Hill, 2022)."

Exercise improves memory function, blood flow, learning abilities, brain plasticity, retention of new mental and physical skills, and how your brain cells communicate with one another. You will also see a boost in your mood because each time you exercise you get a swift kick of dopamine to your brain, which will feel similar to the instant gratification high that you get when you react impulsively (Basso & Suzuki, 2017).

Some of the best exercises for ADHD are below. After you exercise, it's recommended that your journal about how you feel and think so you can see how things are different for you (Preiato, 2021):

- Bicycling

- Spinning

- Jogging

- Hiking

- Browning

- Elliptical

- Boxing

- Martial arts

- HIIT (high-intensity interval training)

- CrossFit

- Weightlifting

ADHD has many symptoms, including mental burnout that causes impulsivity and inattention. Exercises and activities above will help avoid burnout from your ADHD symptoms.

Conclusion

This chapter discussed how healthy eating and exercise could help work out some of your ADHD symptoms and give you more focus and a less foggy ADHD brain. When you include exercises, even walking, into your daily routine, you will attain better memory, blood flow, ability to learn, retention of psychical and mental skills, and brain plasticity. Your mood will also get steadier, and brain cells will communicate more clearly (Basso & Suzuki, 2017).

CONCLUSION

Rewriting the ADHD Script

With everything in this workbook, you have the tools to write your own ADHD script. You are an amazing individual with many incredible qualities. Although ADHD will give you some bumps and bruises along the way, you can challenge each one, flourish, and find the best version of yourself.

Thank You

Before you leave, I'd just like to say, thank you so much for purchasing my book.

I spent many days and nights working on this book so I could finally put this in your hands.

So, before you leave, I'd like to ask you a small favor.

Would you please consider posting a review on the platform? Your reviews are one of the best ways to support indie authors like me, and every review counts.

Your feedback will allow me to continue writing books just like this one, so let me know if you enjoyed it and why. I read every review and I would love to hear from you.